HMH | into **Math**™

Volume 1

Modules 1–9

ISBN 978-1-328-96017-7

7 8 9 10   0877   28 27 26 25 24 23 22 21

4500842462   C D E F G

Dear Students and Families,

Welcome to *Into Math, Grade 4!* In this program, you will develop skills and make sense of mathematics by solving real-world problems, using hands-on tools and strategies, and collaborating with your classmates.

With the support of your teacher and by engaging with meaningful practice, you will learn to persevere when solving problems. *Into Math* will not only help you deepen your understanding of mathematics, but also build your confidence as a learner of mathematics.

Even more exciting, you will write all your ideas and solutions right in your book. In your *Into Math* book, writing and drawing on the pages will help you think deeply about what you are learning, help you truly understand math, and most important, you will become a confident user of mathematics!

Sincerely,
The Authors

Authors

Edward B. Burger, PhD
President, Southwestern University
Georgetown, Texas

Matthew R. Larson, PhD
Past-President, National Council
of Teachers of Mathematics
Lincoln Public Schools
Lincoln, Nebraska

Juli K. Dixon, PhD
Professor, Mathematics Education
University of Central Florida
Orlando, Florida

Steven J. Leinwand
Principal Research Analyst
American Institutes for Research
Washington, DC

Timothy D. Kanold, PhD
Mathematics Educator
Chicago, Illinois

Jennifer Lempp
Educational Consultant
Alexandria, Virginia

Consultants

**English Language
Development Consultant**

Harold Asturias
Director, Center for Mathematics
Excellence and Equity
Lawrence Hall of Science, University of California
Berkeley, California

Program Consultant

David Dockterman, EdD
Lecturer, Harvard Graduate School of Education
Cambridge, Massachusetts

Blended Learning Consultant

Weston Kieschnick
Senior Fellow
International Center for Leadership in Education
Littleton, Colorado

STEM Consultants

Michael A. DiSpezio
Global Educator
North Falmouth, Massachusetts

Marjorie Frank
Science Writer and
Content-Area Reading Specialist
Brooklyn, New York

Bernadine Okoro
Access and Equity and
STEM Learning Advocate and Consultant
Washington, DC

Cary I. Sneider, PhD
Associate Research Professor
Portland State University
Portland, Oregon

Place Value and Whole Number Operations

◗ Build Understanding   ◗ Connect Concepts and Skills   ◗ Apply and Practice

MODULE 2 Addition and Subtraction of Whole Numbers

© Houghton Mifflin Harcourt Publishing Company • Image Credit: (bl)
©Shutterstock; (br) ©Erik Isakson/Alamy

● Build Understanding   ● Connect Concepts and Skills   ● Apply and Practice

Unit 2

Multiplication and Division Problems

© Houghton Mifflin Harcourt Publishing Company • Image Credit:
©PhotosIndia.com LLC/Alamy

Build Understanding   Connect Concepts and Skills   Apply and Practice

MODULE 6 Understand Division by 1-Digit Numbers

Build Understanding   Connect Concepts and Skills   Apply and Practice

MODULE 7 Divide by 1-Digit Numbers

Unit 3 Extend and Apply Multiplication

MODULE 8 Multiply by 2-Digit Numbers

Build Understanding   Connect Concepts and Skills   Apply and Practice

MODULE 9 Apply Multiplication to Area

© Houghton Mifflin Harcourt Publishing Company • Image Credit: (br) ©Pat Canova/Alamy

Build Understanding   Connect Concepts and Skills   Apply and Practice

Place Value and Whole-Number Operations

Musician

STEM POWERING INGENUITY

Each human culture has music, just as each has language. The Bureau of Labor Statistics summarizes that in 2016 there were over 170,000 jobs for musicians and singers in the United States alone. If you include people who play music just for fun, it is reasonable to assume there are millions of musicians in the world.

It is impossible to know exactly how many types of instruments there are, but experts believe the number to be in the thousands. You might already play, or be thinking about playing, an instrument. There is so much to decide! Which instrument will you choose? How much will you practice?

STEM Task:

Work with a partner to gather information about sound. Cut a 4-foot piece of yarn. Tightly tie the handle of a metal spoon to the center of the yarn. Then wrap each end of the yarn around each of your index fingers. Hold your fingers against your ears. Have your partner tap the hanging spoon with a ruler. Try a larger spoon and other types of objects. Collect data about the sound of each object. What can you and your partner infer about sound?

Learning Mindset
Challenge-Seeking Make Decisions

Choosing or accepting any new challenge requires you to make a lot of decisions. Gathering information is one step in a decision-making process. What information can you gather before selecting an instrument to study? You can study different types of music. You can try out different instruments before you choose one. You can also determine if you have enough time to practice.

Reflect

Q What information about sound did you and your partner gather?

Q How did the objects you chose to tie to the yarn affect the sound?

1 Place Value of Whole Numbers

How should I round?

- The eight numbers shown below were accidentally erased from the table.

  729   737   752   768   831   843   858   866

- Write each number in the table to correctly show rounding. Use each number only one time.

Rounded to the Nearest Ten	Original Number	Rounded to the Nearest Hundred
860 ←		
	→	900
730 ←		
	→	700
770 ←		
	→	800
750 ←		
840 ←		

 **Turn and Talk**

- What whole numbers round to 800 when rounded to the nearest ten? to the nearest hundred?

- How can you round 755 to the nearest ten? to the nearest hundred? How do the rounded numbers compare to 755?

Are You Ready?

Complete these problems to review prior concepts and skills you will need for this module.

Tens and Ones

Write the number in three different ways.

1 _____ tens _____ ones

_____ + _____

_____

2 _____ tens _____ ones

_____ + _____

_____

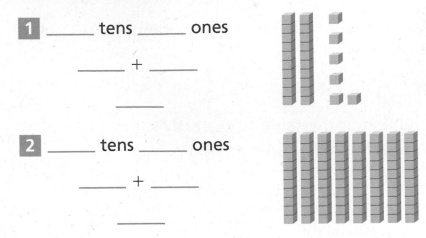

Place Value to One Thousand

Write the value of the underlined digit.

3 1<u>5</u>6 _____

4 <u>9</u>4 _____

5 5<u>0</u>1 _____

6 <u>8</u>46 _____

Regroup Hundreds as Tens

Regroup the hundreds as tens. Write the unknown numbers.

7 300 = _____ tens

8 275 = _____ tens _____ ones

9 793 = _____ tens _____ ones

10 452 = _____ tens _____ ones

11 Circle the greatest number. Explain how you know.

3 hundreds 15 tens   4 hundreds   430

Understand Place Value Relationships

(I Can) use a place-value chart to compare the values of different digits and justify the comparisons.

Spark Your Learning

Some museums keep collections of insect specimens as a historic record. Experts keep track of inventory, inspect specimen cases for damage, and check that labels are set correctly. How can you show the number of beetles in the Museum Insect Inventory?

Show your thinking.

Museum Insect Inventory		
Insect		**Number**
	beetles	1,240
	wasps	19,725
	butterflies	11,100

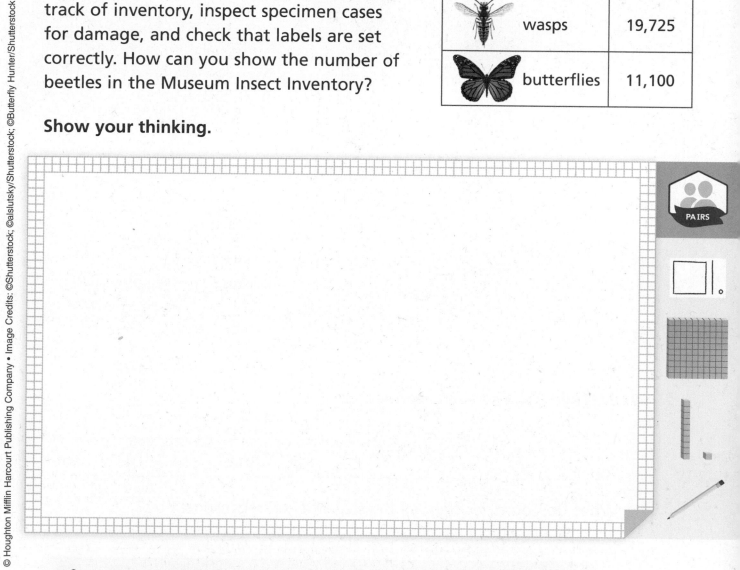

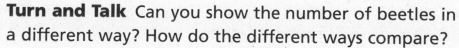

Turn and Talk Can you show the number of beetles in a different way? How do the different ways compare?

Build Understanding

1 The museum has 11,100 butterfly specimens. Describe the relationship between the values of the digits in the thousands place and the hundreds place in 11,100.

Represent and describe ten thousands, thousands, hundreds, tens, and ones.

Blue Mountain Swallowtail butterfly

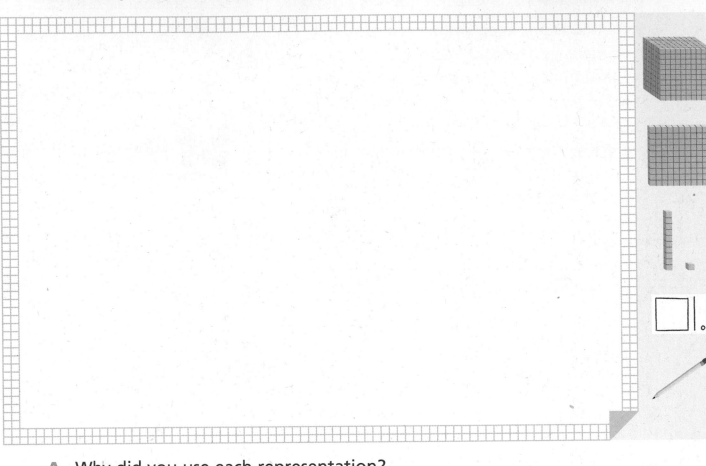

A. Why did you use each representation?

_____

_____

B. What do you notice about the size of each representation?

_____

C. Describe the relationship between the values of the digits in the thousands place and hundreds place in 11,100.

_____

2 As many as 136,080 insect fragments could be found in the foods you buy at the grocery store. This means you might be eating bugs! What is the value of each digit in the number 136,080?

The value of each digit depends on its place-value position. A place-value chart can help you understand the value of each digit in a number.

Write the digits for 136,080 in the top row of the place-value chart.

Connect to Vocabulary

Place value describes the value of a digit in a number.

Each group of three digits in a multi-digit number, separated by commas or spaces, is called a **period**. Each period has Hundreds, Tens, and Ones.

period			period			period		
MILLIONS			THOUSANDS			ONES		
Hundreds	Tens	Ones	Hundreds	Tens	Ones	Hundreds	Tens	Ones
			1 hundred thousand	ten thousands			hundreds		
				30,000				80	

A. What is the place-value position of the digit 6? _____

B. How can you find the value of the digit 1?

_____

C. Write other ways to find the value of the digits in the place-value chart.

D. What do you notice about the value of each place in the place-value chart?

_____

 Turn and Talk How can you use the place-value chart to compare the values of the digits 3 and 6?

Step It Out

3 Yellow jacket wasps live in colonies that can contain up to 15,000 wasps, while bee colonies can have as many as 50,000 bees. How does the value of the digit 5 in 50,000 compare with the value of the digit 5 in 15,000?

Use the place-value chart to compare.

A. Show 15,000. The value of the

digit 5 is _____.

THOUSANDS			ONES		
Hundreds	Tens	Ones	Hundreds	Tens	Ones

B. Show 50,000. The value of the

digit 5 is _____.

THOUSANDS			ONES		
Hundreds	Tens	Ones	Hundreds	Tens	Ones

C. Which digit 5 has the greater

value? _____

D. The value of the digit 5 in 50,000 is _____ times the value of the digit 5 in 15,000.

Turn and Talk What is another way you can compare the digits without using a place-value chart?

Check Understanding 🔲 Math Board

1 There are over 2,000 different species of jellyfish. The largest species have tentacles 200 feet long. How does the value of the digit 2 in 2,000 compare with the value of the digit 2 in 200?

_____

Write the value of the underlined digit.

2 1<u>4</u>,826

3 <u>2</u>75,913

4 <u>7</u>2,658

_____   _____

On Your Own

5 In 2009, experts were called to a Baltimore wastewater treatment plant to remove orb weaving spider webbing. In the web samples that were removed, there were 31,194 spiders. Write the value of the digit 3 in two different ways.

_____

6 (MP) **Use Structure** The praying mantis collection at a museum includes 13,000 specimens, while another museum has a collection of 300 specimens. How many times as great is the value of the digit 3 in 13,000 than the value of the digit 3 in 300?

Orchid mantis

_____

(MP) **Attend to Precision** Write the number in the place-value chart. Then complete the chart to find the value of each digit.

7 23,518

THOUSANDS			ONES		
Hundreds	Tens	Ones	Hundreds	Tens	Ones
		3 thousands			
			500		

8 A beekeeper studies a colony of honeybees that has 1 queen bee, about 250 male drones, and about 37,250 female worker bees. Write the value of the digit 7 in 37,250 in two different ways.

_____

On Your Own

9 One day, a cricket chirps 115,200 times. The next day it chirps 11,020 times. How many times as great is the value of the digit 2 in 115,200 than the value of the digit 2 in 11,020? How do you know?

_____

Write the digit in its place-value position.

10 5,619

_____ thousands

_____ hundreds

_____ tens

_____ ones

11 605,981

_____ hundred thousands

_____ ten thousands

_____ thousands

_____ hundreds

_____ tens

_____ ones

(MP) **Attend to Precision** Compare the values of the underlined digits. Then complete the sentence.

12 <u>2</u>6,451 and <u>2</u>,385   The value of the digit 2 in _____ is _____ times

the value of the digit 2 in _____.

13 <u>3</u>,000 and <u>3</u>0,000   The value of the digit 3 in _____ is _____ times

the value of the digit 3 in _____.

I'm in a Learning Mindset!

How does my mindset affect my confidence when I compare the relationships between the place-value positions?

_____

Name _____

Read and Write Numbers

(I Can) read and write 6-digit numbers in standard form, word form, and expanded form.

Spark Your Learning

The total area of Texas is two hundred sixty-eight thousand, five hundred ninety-six square miles. It is the largest state in the southern U.S. How can you write the total area of Texas in two different ways using numbers?

Show your thinking.

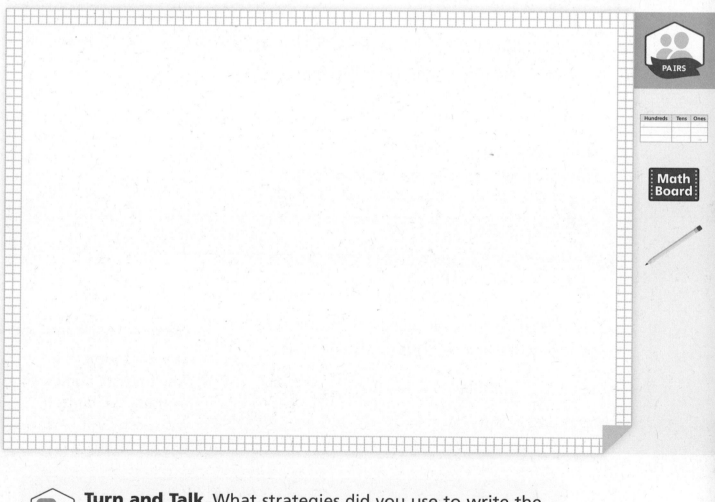

Turn and Talk What strategies did you use to write the total area in two different ways using numbers? Describe how your ways are related.

Build Understanding

1 The distance through Earth from one side to the other at the equator, in miles, is shown using base-ten blocks.

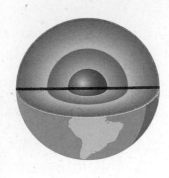

Use what you know about place value to write the number in the place-value chart.

THOUSANDS			ONES		
Hundreds	Tens	Ones	Hundreds	Tens	Ones

A. How can you use what you know about place value to write the number in standard form?

_____

_____

_____

B. The distance through Earth from one side to the other at the equator, in miles, is

_____ miles.

 Turn and Talk How can you use period names and commas to write the number?

Step It Out

2 The speed of light is 186,282 miles per second.

A. Write the number in the place-value chart.

THOUSANDS			ONES		
Hundreds	Tens	Ones	Hundreds	Tens	Ones

B. Use the place-value chart to help you read and write the number in word form. Use a comma to separate periods. _____

_____

C. Write the value of each digit.

_____

D. Use the value of each digit to write the number in expanded form.

_____ + _____ + _____ + _____ + _____ + _____

Turn and Talk How is the expanded form of 186,282 related to its standard form?

Connect to Vocabulary

In **word form**, write numbers by using words.

In **expanded form**, write numbers by writing the sum of the values of each of the digits.

Check Understanding

1 An article in the local newspaper states that 10,973 cans of food were collected for the community food pantry. How can you write 10,973 in expanded form?

_____

2 Write the number in a different form.

30,000 + 400 + 50 _____

On Your Own

3 **MP** **Attend to Precision** The deepest part of the ocean, the Mariana Trench, is 35,462 feet deep. How would you write this number in word form?

_____

Write the number in expanded form.

4 4,902

5 seven hundred thousand, four hundred

6 **STEM** Phosphate is mined from rock minerals to make fertilizer. Florida has the largest known phosphate deposits in the United States. The Florida phosphate industry owns or has rights to about 443,210 acres of land. How can you write 443,210 in expanded form and word form?

_____

Write the number in standard form.
Use the place-value chart to help you.

THOUSANDS			ONES		
Hundreds	Tens	Ones	Hundreds	Tens	Ones

7 seventy thousand, four hundred sixty-eight

8 A cruise is four hundred twenty-four thousand, eight hundred seconds long. What is the length of the cruise written in standard form?

_____

© Houghton Mifflin Harcourt Publishing Company

➗ I'm in a Learning Mindset!

Did I face any new challenges?

_____

Name

Regroup and Rename Numbers

(I Can) regroup and rename multi-digit whole numbers.

Spark Your Learning

There are about 18,500 known species of butterflies in the world.

Zebra Longwing butterfly

Show how you can regroup and rename the number 18,500 in five different ways.

 Turn and Talk Why can you regroup and rename 18,500 in another way?

Build Understanding

1 The North American Butterfly Association runs about 450 Butterfly Counts. Each year, volunteers count all of the butterflies observed within a 15-mile count circle in a one-day period. For this year's count, Dr. Fiona ordered 1,700 pencils.

Show 1,700 using a large cube and flats. Then draw a quick picture to show your work.

A. What is another name for 1,700 using thousands and hundreds?

_____

Connect to Vocabulary

When you **regroup** a number, you exchange amounts of equal value to rename a number.

B. If you regroup the thousands cube as flats, how many flats would you need?

_____

C. How many flats do you need to rename 1,700 as hundreds?

_____

D. How can you rename 1,700 as hundreds?

_____

Turn and Talk Why do the two names represent the same number, 1,700?

Step It Out

2 Dr. Fiona also needs 100,000 recording sheets for the Butterfly Count. How can you use a place-value chart to regroup and rename 100,000?

Grass Yellow butterfly

A. Write 100,000 in the place-value chart.

B. Use the place-value chart to help you regroup and rename the number in each place-value position.

THOUSANDS			ONES		
Hundreds	Tens	Ones	Hundreds	Tens	Ones

____1____ hundred thousands

_____ ten thousands

_____ thousands

_____ hundreds

_____ tens

_____ ones

Turn and Talk What do you notice about the value of each position as you move left on the place-value chart?

• •

Check Understanding [Math Board]

Use the place-value chart to help you regroup and rename the number.

1 23 ten thousands = _____ hundreds

2 23 ten thousands = _____ thousands

3 23 ten thousands = _____ tens

THOUSANDS			ONES		
Hundreds	Tens	Ones	Hundreds	Tens	Ones

On Your Own

4 Jenna used base-ten blocks to show that 2,400 people went to a swim meet. How can you regroup and rename 2,400?

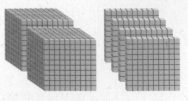

2,400 = _____ hundreds

5 **Open Ended** Adrian split up Jenna's base-ten blocks to show half the number of people that went to the swim meet. How can you regroup and rename half of 2,400?

_____

Regroup and rename the number 520,000. Use the place-value chart to help.

THOUSANDS			ONES		
Hundreds	Tens	Ones	Hundreds	Tens	Ones

6 520,000 = 520 _____

Regroup and rename the number.

7 490 = _____ tens

8 560,000 = 56 _____

9 (MP) **Attend to Precision** Students at a school collected 11,000 cans of food for the community food pantry. They can pack the cans in boxes of 100 to take them to the pantry. How many boxes will they need to pack all of the cans? _____

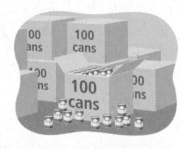

I'm in a Learning Mindset!

What challenges do I face when regrouping and renaming numbers?

_____

_____

Name _____

Compare and Order Numbers

(I Can) compare and order three numbers to the hundred thousands place. I can record and justify the comparisons.

Spark Your Learning

The Library of Congress, in Washington, D.C., is the largest library in the world. It has about 700,000 rare books, about 124,000 telephone books, and about 140,000 comic books. How can you compare the numbers to find out which kind of book there is the most of at the Library of Congress?

Show your thinking.

SMALL GROUPS

Hundreds	Tens	Ones

Math Board

The Library of Congress has the most _____.

Turn and Talk How do you know your answer is correct?

Build Understanding

1 Biscayne National Park is the largest marine park in the national park system. If you visit, be prepared to get wet because 95% of the park is underwater. Each year, visitors explore coral reefs, islands, and mangrove forests. In which year did more visitors come to the park?

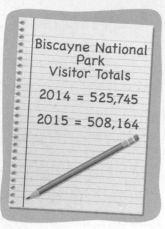

Biscayne National Park
Visitor Totals

2014 = 525,745

2015 = 508,164

A. How can you compare the numbers?

_____

_____

Write the number of visitors for each year in the place-value chart.

THOUSANDS			ONES		
Hundreds	Tens	Ones	Hundreds	Tens	Ones

B. Where do you start when you compare the numbers?

_____

C. How can you compare the digits?

_____

_____

_____

D. During which year did more visitors come to Biscayne

National Park? _____

Turn and Talk Why can you use a place-value chart to compare numbers?

Step It Out

2 In 2016, there were 514,709 visitors to Biscayne National Park. Use the number line to order the number of visitors to the park in 2014, 2015, and 2016 from least to greatest.

A. Locate and label the points on the number line that represent the number of visitors each year.

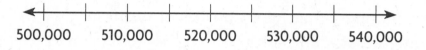

500,000   510,000   520,000   530,000   540,000

B. Write the number of visitors for each year in order from least to greatest.

_____

C. Compare the number of visitors in 2014 and 2016. Write <, >, or =.

525,745 ◯ 514,709

 Turn and Talk How can you compare and order three numbers at one time?

Check Understanding 【Math Board】

Compare. Write <, >, or =. Use the number line to help.

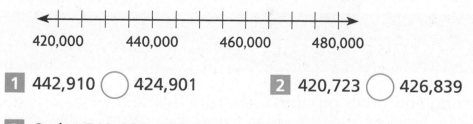

420,000   440,000   460,000   480,000

1 442,910 ◯ 424,901   **2** 420,723 ◯ 426,839

3 Order 712,896, 702,486, and 727,894 from greatest to least.

_____

On Your Own

4 (MP) **Reason** How can you compare the values of the underlined digits in the number 3<u>22</u>,179?

_____

_____

5 **Open Ended** Riley writes the number 840,361. Trevor uses the same digits to write a number greater than Riley's number. Jackson uses the same digits to write a number that is less than the numbers that Riley and Trevor wrote. What number could each student write?

Riley: _____   Trevor: _____   Jackson: _____

Compare. Write <, >, or =.

6 109,687 ◯ 190,678   **7** 587,381 ◯ 587,318   **8** 225,976 ◯ 225,976

9 The students in Mrs. Edwards' class participate in a 40 Book Challenge every school year. After they record their book titles, they find the total number of pages read. How can you compare and order the number of pages read from least to greatest?

40 Book Challenge		
	Number of books	Number of pages read
Owen	24	8,532
Lucy	25	8,642
Tara	24	8,465

_____

_____

➗ I'm in a Learning Mindset!

How will I use comparing and ordering numbers in the future?

_____

_____

© Houghton Mifflin Harcourt Publishing Company

Name _____

Use Place Value Understanding to Round Numbers

(I Can) use place-value understanding to round whole numbers through 1,000,000 and estimate.

Spark Your Learning

In a class discussion, Anja says the total area of Alaska is about 700,000 square miles when rounded to the nearest hundred thousand. Liam says the total area of Alaska is about 660,000 square miles when rounded to the nearest ten thousand. Mr. D'Andrea says they are both right. What can be the actual total area of Alaska?

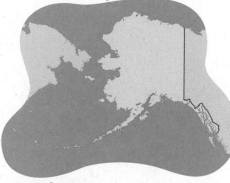

Total area of Alaska = ■ **square miles**

Show your thinking.

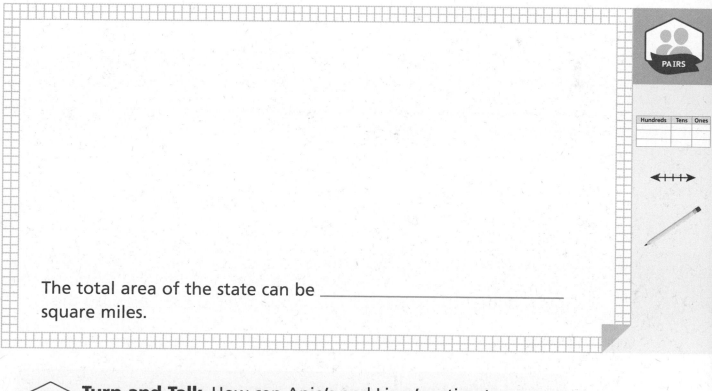

The total area of the state can be _____ square miles.

Turn and Talk How can Anja's and Liam's estimates of the total area both be right?

Build Understanding

1 An organization is collecting spare change to donate to local charities. For the month of June, they collected 12,678 coins. About how many coins, rounded to the nearest ten thousand, were collected in June?

A. How can you use place value to round a number to the nearest ten thousand?

_____

_____

B. How can you use a number line to round a number to the nearest ten thousand?

_____

C. Between which two ten thousands is the number of coins collected for June? _____

D. How can using the number line and halfway point tell you which ten thousand the number of coins collected for June is closer to?

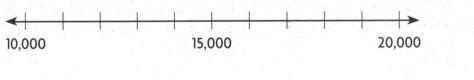

10,000   15,000   20,000

_____

_____

E. 12,678 is closer to _____ than _____.

F. 12,678 rounded to the nearest ten thousand is _____, so the organization collected about _____ coins in June.

Turn and Talk Why can you use rounding as a way to estimate?

Step It Out

2 When the coin collection period ends, there are 26,411 coins. How can you round 26,411 to the nearest thousand?

Use place value to round 26,411 to the nearest thousand.

A. To round a number to the nearest thousand, find the thousands it is between.

_____ < 26,411 < _____

B. Look at the digit in the place-value position to the right of the rounding place. Circle it.

If the digit is 5 or greater, the digit in the rounding place increases by 1.

C. The digit in the hundreds place is _____,

so _____ is closer to _____ than _____.

D. 26,411 rounded to the nearest thousand is _____.

Turn and Talk Why would your answer change if the number of coins were 26,511 instead of 26,411?

Check Understanding · Math Board

1 A restaurant serves 17,236 customers in May. To the nearest thousand, how many customers does the restaurant serve?

_____

Draw a number line or use place value to round to the place value of the underlined digit.

2 4<u>3</u>9,168

_____

3 47<u>6</u>,168

_____

On Your Own

4 **Geography** The state of New York has a total area of 54,555 square miles. What is the total area of New York rounded to the nearest ten thousand square miles?

_____

5 (MP) **Reason** A growing design company is hoping to make enough money this quarter to buy an office space that costs $735,495. Explain why the financial officer would round the cost of the space to $800,000.

_____

_____

_____

6 **Open Ended** The population of a city is about 600,000 when the actual population is rounded to the nearest hundred thousand. When that actual population is rounded to the nearest ten thousand, the estimated population is 580,000. Write five numbers that could be the actual population of this city.

_____

Round to the place value of the underlined digit.

7 6̲18,287

8 583̲,507

9 25̲6,565

_____ _____ _____

I'm in a Learning Mindset!

What can I do to support the success of others when rounding numbers?

_____

_____

Vocabulary

Choose the correct term from the Vocabulary box to complete the sentence.

Vocabulary
estimate
expanded form
place value
period
regroup
round
standard form
word form

1 The _____ of 512,789 is
500,000 + 10,000 + 2,000 + 700 + 80 + 9.

2 When you _____ a number,
you exchange amounts of equal value to
rename the number.

3 _____ describes the value of a digit
in a number, based on the location of the digit.

Concepts and Skills

4 (MP) **Use Tools** Select all of the ways to regroup and
rename 4,200. State which strategy or tool you will use to
answer the question, explain your choice, and then select
the answers.

   Ⓐ 42 hundreds   Ⓓ 420 tens

   Ⓑ 42 thousands   Ⓔ 420 ones

   Ⓒ 4,200 ones   Ⓕ 420 thousands

_____

_____

5 Which is the correct value that completes the sentence?

The value of the digit 2 in 321,705 is ■ times the value of
the digit 2 in 32,571.

   Ⓐ 10   Ⓑ 100   Ⓒ 1,000   Ⓓ 10,000

6 What is $200{,}000 + 80{,}000 + 500 + 70 + 1$ written in standard form?

_____

7 In the United States, about 620,000 dogs that enter animal shelters as strays are returned to their owners. Which numbers round to 620,000 when rounded to the nearest ten thousand? Select all that apply.

Ⓐ 619,000

Ⓑ 605,000

Ⓒ 621,000

Ⓓ 625,000

Ⓔ 614,000

8 Which comparison is true? Select all that apply.

Ⓐ $37{,}940 > 37{,}939$

Ⓑ $473{,}248 = 473{,}248$

Ⓒ $16{,}105 = 16{,}103$

Ⓓ $801{,}269 > 801{,}296$

Ⓔ $37{,}340 < 37{,}890$

9 Which shows the numbers ordered correctly from least to greatest? Select all that apply.

Ⓐ 32,245; 32,452; 32,425

Ⓑ 304,561; 305,561; 306,561

Ⓒ 817,902; 871,029; 871,092

Ⓓ 216,135; 261,532; 216,153

Ⓔ 86,109; 96,869; 169,715

Addition and Subtraction of Whole Numbers

How **can** you reason in **reverse**?

- A filmmaker wants to record scenes on the roofs of three buildings. She uses a drone with a camera.

- Suppose the drone starts on the roof of one building, flies down to the roof of a second building, and then flies up to land on a third building, as shown.

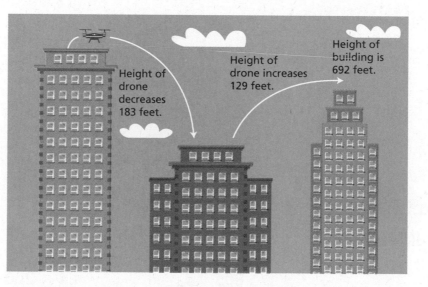

Height of drone decreases 183 feet.

Height of drone increases 129 feet.

Height of building is 692 feet.

- How tall is the first building? _____

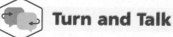 **Turn and Talk**

- How does the relationship between addition and subtraction help you solve this problem?

ONLINE ⊙Ed

Are You Ready?

Complete these problems to review prior concepts and skills you will need for this module.

Column Addition

Circle two addends to add first. Then find the sum.

1
```
  6
  2
+ 4
```

2
```
  3
  5
  5
+ 1
```

3
```
  8
  7
  2
+ 3
```

Two-Digit Addition and Subtraction

Find the sum or difference.

4
```
  16
+ 35
```

5
```
  84
- 56
```

6
```
  67
+ 29
```

Subtract Through 3-Digit Numbers

Find the difference.

7
```
  591
-   7
```

8
```
  805
-  26
```

9
```
  200
-  46
```

10 Selena had 806 marbles in a jar. She gave Taryn 109 marbles from the jar. How many marbles does Selena have left in the jar?

_____

Name

Add Whole Numbers and Assess Reasonableness

(I Can) add whole numbers greater than 1,000 using place value and a grid with regrouping.

Spark Your Learning

In 2016, Washington's Port Townsend-Coupeville ferry had about 329 thousand vehicle passengers and about 118 thousand foot passengers. How many passengers rode the ferry in 2016? How can you write this using numbers only?

Show your thinking.

Turn and Talk Why would an estimate instead of an exact answer be a reasonable solution to this problem?

Build Understanding

1 In 2015, North Dakota reported 545,027 licensed drivers, and Wyoming reported 422,450 licensed drivers. How many licensed drivers were there in both states? Use rounding as a strategy to show your answer is reasonable.

Use the grid to help you solve the problem.

	Hundred Thousands	Ten Thousands	Thousands	Hundreds	Tens	Ones
+						

There were _____ licensed drivers in both states.

A. Round each addend to the nearest ten thousand and then add. Show your work.

_____

About how many total licensed drivers were there in 2015?

_____

Connect to Vocabulary

To **estimate** is to find an answer that is close to the exact amount.

B. Does your estimate show your answer is reasonable? Explain.

_____

_____

Turn and Talk How can you use a grid as a place-value chart to help you add greater numbers?

Step It Out

2 In January, 611,749 domestic passengers and 106,909 international passengers departed or arrived at Terminal 4 of the airport. What number of passengers departed or arrived at Terminal 4 in January?

Estimate. Then find the sum.

A. Round the numbers to the nearest hundred thousand. Then add.

_____

B. Use the grid to help you align the addends by place value. Find the sum.

In January, _____ passengers arrived or departed at Terminal 4.

C. Compare your sum to your estimate. Is your answer reasonable? Explain.

_____

Check Understanding [Math Board]

1 A company's buses make 480,000 trips. A second company's buses make 44,100 trips. How many trips do the two

companies' buses make? _____

Estimate. Then find the sum.

2 Estimate: _____

$$\begin{array}{r} 319{,}587 \\ +\ 167{,}259 \\ \hline \end{array}$$

3 Estimate: _____

$$\begin{array}{r} 9{,}114 \\ +\ 5{,}697 \\ \hline \end{array}$$

4 Estimate: _____

$$\begin{array}{r} 82{,}349 \\ +\ 16{,}624 \\ \hline \end{array}$$

On Your Own

5 (MP) **Construct Arguments** During a year, 580,242 vehicle passengers and 299,860 foot passengers ride on a ferry. How many passengers ride the ferry that year? Explain how you know your answer is reasonable.

_____

_____

_____

6 (MP) **Use Structure** The daily average number of bus passengers for different local routes is shown. How many bus passengers are there daily?

Bus Routes	
Local Routes	**Number of Passengers**
Red	124,707
Green	358,305
Blue	94,535

_____

Estimate. Then find the sum.

7 Estimate: _____

$$
\begin{array}{r}
1,223 \\
+\ 2,009 \\
\hline
\end{array}
$$

8 Estimate: _____

$$
\begin{array}{r}
609,987 \\
+\ 123,654 \\
\hline
\end{array}
$$

9 Estimate: _____

$$
\begin{array}{r}
99,852 \\
+\ 27,415 \\
\hline
\end{array}
$$

10 **Open Ended** Write and solve a real-world problem using 461,283 and 215,079 as addends.

_____

_____

_____

I'm in a Learning Mindset!

Did using a grid help me add greater numbers? How?

_____

© Houghton Mifflin Harcourt Publishing Company

Name _____

Subtract Whole Numbers and Assess Reasonableness

(I Can) subtract whole numbers greater than 1,000 using place value and a grid with regrouping.

Spark Your Learning

Biologists classify living things on Earth by kingdoms. The approximate number of species in two different kingdoms are shown. How many more fungi species are there than plant species?

Write the difference using only numbers.

Approximate Number of Species per Kingdom	
Kingdom	Number of Species
Fungi	611 thousand
Plants	298 thousand

SMALL GROUPS

Hundreds	Tens	Ones

Turn and Talk How did you know that you needed to regroup some of the place values?

Build Understanding

1 A natural history museum has 102,248 spider and scorpion specimens and 10,425 bird specimens. How many more spider and scorpion specimens are there than bird specimens?

Use the grid to help you solve the problem.

A. How can you use subtraction to solve this problem?

_____

_____

_____

B. Which place value should you

start with when subtracting? _____

C. Subtract to find the answer.

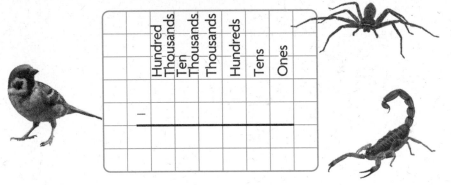

D. Which place values did you regroup?

_____

E. Use rounding to estimate the answer. Does your estimate show your answer is reasonable? Explain.

_____

_____

Turn and Talk Does the estimated difference being close to your answer mean your answer is correct? Explain.

Step It Out

2 Of the 41,415 plant and animal species on a conservation group's endangered species list, 16,306 are listed as near extinction. How many of the species on the list are not considered near extinction?

A. Estimate. Round to the nearest ten thousand.

Then subtract. _____

B. Use the grid to record the problem.

C. Subtract the ones.

Continue to subtract by place value.
What place values need to be regrouped?

_____

There are _____ species considered endangered but not yet near extinction.

D. Does your estimate show your answer is reasonable? Explain.

_____

Check Understanding 〔Math Board〕

1 A scientific database lists 7,858 species of amphibians, and another database lists 5,513 species of mammals. How many more amphibian species than mammal species are listed?

There are _____ more amphibian species listed than mammal species.

Estimate. Then find the difference.

2 Estimate: _____

$$\begin{array}{r} 518,112 \\ -\ 295,763 \\ \hline \end{array}$$

3 Estimate: _____

$$\begin{array}{r} 567,023 \\ -\ 48,911 \\ \hline \end{array}$$

4 Estimate: _____

$$\begin{array}{r} 5,760 \\ -\ 2,695 \\ \hline \end{array}$$

On Your Own

5 **STEM** At present, the highest peak of the Appalachian Mountains is 6,684 feet. Millions of years ago, before weathering and erosion had occurred, the highest peak was about 30,000 feet. What is the difference between the highest peak millions of years ago and the highest peak today? Explain how you know your answer is reasonable.

_____

_____

6 **(MP) Use Structure** Some biologists predict that there are about 27,500 species in the kingdom chromista and 36,400 species in the kingdom protozoa. How many more species of protozoa are predicted to exist than species of

chromista? _____

Estimate. Then find the difference.

7 Estimate: _____

   460,112
− 201,998

8 Estimate: _____

   8,000
− 2,543

9 Estimate: _____

   88,741
− 16,304

10 **Open Ended** Write and solve a problem that requires finding the difference between 68,324 and 12,608.

_____

_____

🔷 I'm in a Learning Mindset!

How did subtracting greater numbers challenge me?

_____

Name _____

Use Addition and Subtraction to Solve Comparison Problems

(I Can) draw a bar model for a comparison problem. I can write an equation and use addition or subtraction to find the unknown number in the bar model.

Spark Your Learning

Mr. Jones set up a savings account to save for a new car. How much more money does he have to save to cover the cost of the car shown?

Draw a visual representation of this problem. Then solve the problem.

Car for Sale
$18,469

New car fund

$3,553

SMALL GROUPS

Hundreds	Tens	Ones

 Turn and Talk How did you decide which operation to use to solve the problem?

Build Understanding

1 A large shopping mall has 10,972 employees for most of the year. During the busy season, the mall has 2,135 more employees. How many employees does the mall have during the busy season?

A. Draw a visual representation of this problem.

B. Write an equation to model the problem. Use *n* for the unknown number. Then solve.

There are _____ employees during the busy season.

 Turn and Talk Compare the equation you wrote to solve the problem with the equations written by your classmates. How are the equations the same? How are they different?

Step It Out

2 On Saturday and Sunday, there were a total of 16,096 mall employees working. On Saturday, there were 8,946 mall employees working. How many fewer mall employees were working on Sunday than on Saturday?

A. Write an equation modeling the number of mall employees, *s*, working Sunday. Find *s*.

_____

B. Write an equation modeling the difference, *w*, in number of mall employees working Sunday and the number working on Saturday. Then find *w*.

_____

C. How can you tell if your answer is reasonable? Explain.

_____

_____

_____

Check Understanding [Math Board]

1 A park had 4,307 visitors on Thursday and 1,614 more visitors on Friday than on Thursday. How many visitors did the park have on Friday?

_____

2 A theater sold 2,149 tickets on opening weekend. By the end of the second weekend, they had sold a total of 5,036 weekend tickets. How many fewer tickets were sold on the opening weekend than on the second weekend?

_____

On Your Own

3 (MP) **Model with Mathematics** The distance from Miami, Florida, to Minneapolis, Minnesota, is 1,793 miles. The distance from Miami to Seattle, Washington, is 3,336 miles. How many more miles is it from Miami to Seattle than it is from Miami to Minneapolis? Write an equation and solve the problem.

_____

_____

4 Mel's Café is open 7 hours a day for 8 days. Mary's Café is open 8 hours a day for 6 days. Which café is open fewer hours? How many fewer hours? Show your work.

_____

5 **Open Ended** A male African elephant weighs 12,218 pounds. A female African elephant weighs 7,376 pounds.

Write a comparison problem using this information. Draw a visual model for your problem. Write an equation and then solve the problem.

_____

_____

© Houghton Mifflin Harcourt Publishing Company • Image Credit: ©Houghton Mifflin Harcourt

⚡ I'm in a **Learning Mindset!**

How could I solve Problem 4 a different way?

_____

Name

Apply the Perimeter Formula for Rectangles

(I Can) apply the perimeter formula to find the perimeter of a rectangle.

Step It Out

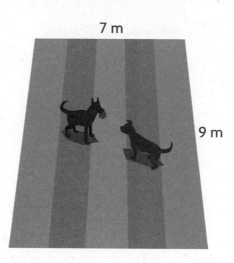

7 m

9 m

1 ▶ Tom and Mary drew plans for a rectangular dog park in their neighborhood. How many meters of fencing would they need to go around the dog park?

The formula below can be used to find the perimeter of a rectangle.

Perimeter $= P = l + w + l + w$

A. What are the values for l and w?

$l =$ _____ meters

$w =$ _____ meters

B. Replace l and w in the formula for perimeter with their values.

$P =$ _____ $+$ _____ $+$ _____ $+$ _____

C. Calculate to find the value of P.

$P =$ _____

D. Solve the problem.

Tom and Mary need _____ meters of fencing.

 Turn and Talk How could you write the formula for the perimeter of a rectangle and the formula for the perimeter of a square using multiplication?

Step It Out

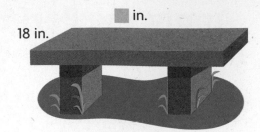

18 in.

■ in.

2 Sandy wants to put a rectangular bench by the fountain. She wants the length to be 3 times the width. What is the perimeter of the bench top?

A. What is width of the bench? _____ inches

B. Use what the problem tells you about how the length relates to the width and find the length of the bench.

length = _____ × width

= _____ × _____ = _____

length = _____ inches

C. What is the perimeter of the bench top? Show your work.

_____

 Turn and Talk How could you find the length if you were only given the perimeter and the width of a rectangle?

Check Understanding ꡐMath Boardꡐ

1 Eric wants to buy a string of lights to go around his window. His window has a width of 4 feet and a length that is 2 feet longer than its width. How many feet of lights should Eric buy?

_____

2 A fence can prevent animals from eating the vegetable garden. What is the least amount of fencing needed to surround the garden?

7 m

| Vegetable Garden | 4 m |

_____

On Your Own

3 (MP) **Use Structure** The new state park will have a rectangular shape with a length of 6 miles and a width of 3 miles. What is the perimeter of the park?

_____

4 (MP) **Use Structure** Zach is training to run a marathon. His practice route is the shape of a square that is 8 kilometers in one direction. How far does Zach run in his practice route?

_____

5 (MP) **Reason** Ashley wants to build a new rectangular pen for her pet rabbit. She knows the perimeter of the new pen will be 40 feet. She also knows that the length can only be 12 feet. What is the width of her new rabbit pen? Explain your thinking.

_____

_____

_____

6 The dimensions for a new wildflower garden are shown. A rope will be placed around the perimeter of the rectangular garden until the seeds have sprouted and bloomed. What is the least amount of rope needed to go around the perimeter of the garden?

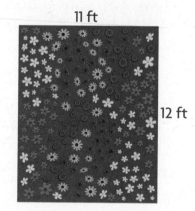

11 ft

12 ft

_____

7 (MP) **Attend to Precision** Find the perimeter of a rectangle if the width is 10 inches and the length is 2 times the width. Explain your thinking.

_____

_____

On Your Own

8 (MP) **Use Structure** Carson is trying out for the football team. He practices drills in a small rectangular field that is 10 yards wide and 11 yards long. What is the perimeter of the field that Carson practices on?

_____

9 (MP) **Model with Mathematics** The school wants to build a small dance floor in their auditorium. The perimeter of the new dance floor will be 44 yards. The length can only be 12 yards. What is the width of their new dance floor? Write an equation and show how you solved the problem.

_____

_____

_____

_____

10 (MP) **Use Structure** The dimensions for Diane's rectangular vegetable garden are shown. She wants to put a border around the garden. How many feet of border does Diane need?

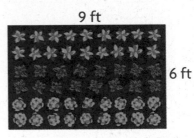

9 ft

6 ft

_____

11 (MP) **Reason** Find the perimeter of a rectangle if the width is 6 centimeters and the length is 5 centimeters longer than the width. Explain your thinking.

_____

_____

_____

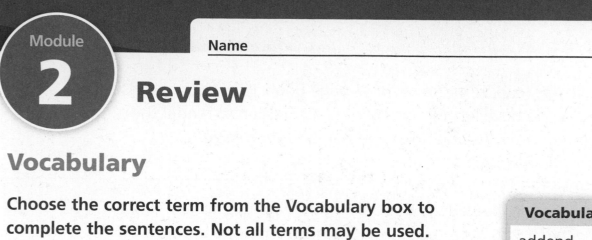
Review

Vocabulary

Choose the correct term from the Vocabulary box to complete the sentences. Not all terms may be used.

Vocabulary

addend

estimate

formula

1 A mathematical relationship expressed in symbols is

called a _____ .

2 A number that is added to another number is called an

_____ .

Concepts and Skills

Estimate. Then find the sum.

3 Estimate: _____
$$480,321$$
$$+ 341,569$$

4 Estimate: _____
$$403,977$$
$$+ 184,952$$

5 Estimate: _____
$$7,784$$
$$+ 2,389$$

Estimate. Then find the difference.

6 Estimate: _____
$$5,000$$
$$- 2,642$$

7 Estimate: _____
$$475,837$$
$$- 264,822$$

8 Estimate: _____
$$68,652$$
$$- 16,867$$

9 (MP) **Use Tools** The sports arena had a total attendance of 54,927 people on Friday and Saturday night. If 23,380 people were in attendance on Saturday night, how many people were in attendance on Friday night? How many more people were in attendance on Friday night than on Saturday night? Tell what strategy or tool you will use to solve the problem, explain your choice, and then find the answers.

_____

_____

10 Gloria has read 57 pages of an 86-page book. How many pages does Gloria have left to read? Write an equation to model the problem. Use *n* for the unknown number. Then solve.

_____

11 The library collected 2,532 books on Friday. The library collected 1,286 more books on Saturday than the amount collected on Friday.

How many books were collected on Saturday? Draw a visual model for this problem. Then solve.

_____

12 Find the perimeter of a rectangle if the width is 3 centimeters and the length is 6 centimeters longer than the width. Explain your thinking.

_____

_____

13 A bike club is planning their training route. The route follows the perimeter of a rectangular park with a length of 5 miles and a width of 4 miles. How far is their route?

Ⓐ 36 miles

Ⓑ 20 miles

Ⓒ 18 miles

Ⓓ 9 miles

14 The diagram shows the plan of the new rectangular playground. How many yards of fencing will the city need if they put a fence around the playground?

_____

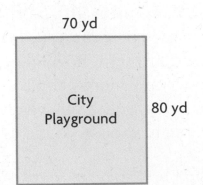

70 yd

City Playground

80 yd

Multiplication and Division Problems

Teacher

STEM
POWERING INGENUITY

Some people say that teachers have the most important job in the world! Almost everyone can tell you about a teacher who changed their lives for the better.

U.S. Presidents Lyndon Johnson and Barack Obama were both teachers.

Have you heard of Helen Keller? Helen Keller was deaf and blind. Anne Sullivan was Helen Keller's teacher. She spelled out words in Helen's hand so that Helen would know that things had words attached to them. Helen later became a successful writer and lecturer.

STEM Task:

People in schools sometimes use a lot of paper. Keep track of how many sheets of paper you use in one school day. Then estimate how much paper all of your classmates use in a day. Go estimate how much paper everyone in your school uses in a day, a month, and a year. Show how you came up with your estimates. Discuss with other students ways people in your school could use less paper.

Learning Mindset
Strategic Help-Seeking
Identifies Need for Help

© Houghton Mifflin Harcourt Publishing Company • Image Credit: ©Monkey Business Images/Shutterstockk

Everyone gets stuck sometimes. The first step in getting unstuck is knowing when you need help. Here are some tips.

- When a task is difficult, stop and think about what makes it challenging. Ask yourself: Do I have the information I need? Do I understand the directions or steps?

- Use those answers to find a source of help. Can I use a tool? Is there another strategy? Should I ask a classmate? Can I look something up?

- Be honest with yourself. Is there a skill you need to improve? Talk to someone else who had to work to improve that skill.

Reflect

Q Do you know when you need help? Do you know when you can help yourself or when you need to ask others?

Q How can you help others?

Interpret and Solve Problem Situations

How can YOU get to 20?

- Use the arrays to write three division equations so that the sum of the three quotients is 20.

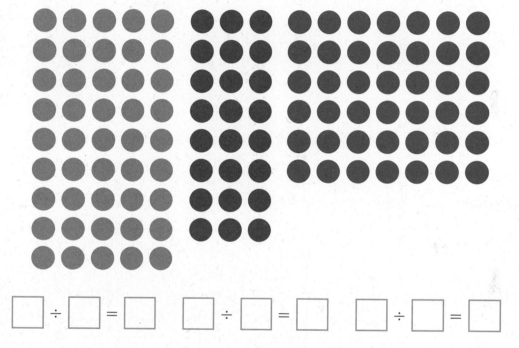

$$\boxed{} \div \boxed{} = \boxed{} \qquad \boxed{} \div \boxed{} = \boxed{} \qquad \boxed{} \div \boxed{} = \boxed{}$$

$$\boxed{} + \boxed{} + \boxed{} = 20$$

 Turn and Talk

- Write a sentence that involves sharing objects among your friends using an array.

- How can you change the equations so that the sum of the quotients is the greatest possible amount?

Are You Ready?

Complete these problems to review prior concepts and skills you will need for this module.

Practice Multiplication Facts

Use multiplication strategies and properties to find the product.

1 $5 \times 4 =$ _____

2 $6 \times 7 =$ _____

3 $9 \times 6 =$ _____

4 $4 \times 3 =$ _____

$3 \times 4 =$ _____

5 $3 \times 2 \times 5 =$ _____

$6 \times 5 =$ _____

6 $5 \times 2 \times 3 =$ _____

$10 \times 3 =$ _____

Meaning of Multiplication: Equal Groups

Complete.

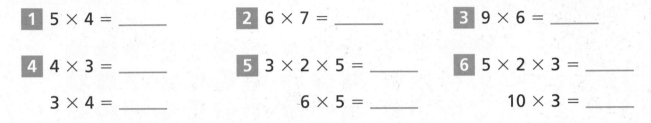

7 _____ groups of _____ = _____

_____ $\times$ _____ = _____

8 _____ jumps of _____ = _____

_____ $\times$ _____ = _____

Meaning of Multiplication: Arrays

Complete.

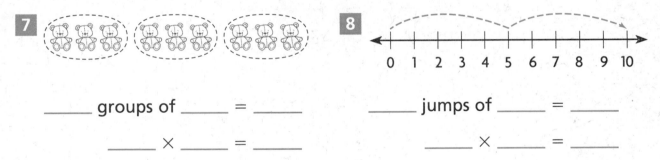

9 _____ rows of _____ = _____

_____ $\times$ _____ = _____

10 _____ rows of _____ = _____

_____ $\times$ _____ = _____

Name

Explore Multiplicative Comparisons

(I Can) use visual models and equations to represent and interpret a multiplicative comparison.

Spark Your Learning

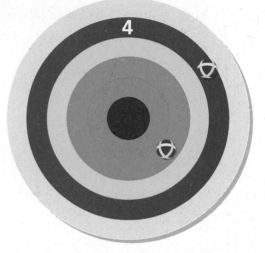

Jaslene throws 2 balls at the target. She gets 4 points for landing on red. She gets 3 times as many points for landing on green.

Use a visual model to show how many points Jaslene gets for landing on red. Then show how many points she gets for landing on green.

PAIRS

Turn and Talk How does your visual model show *3 times as many as 4?* How could you use a different visual model to show the same comparison?

Build Understanding

1 Tomás unlocks 2 levels in a video game. Sasha unlocks 5 times as many levels as Tomás. How many levels does Sasha unlock?

Use a visual model to represent the problem.

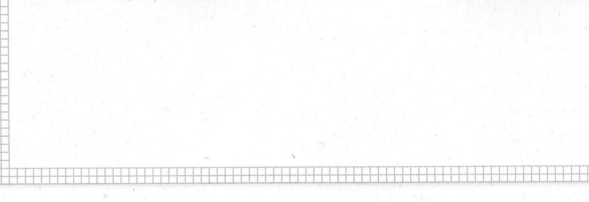

A. How does your visual model show the number of levels Tomás unlocks?

_____

B. How does your visual model show that Sasha unlocks 5 times as many levels as Tomás?

_____

_____

C. Complete the comparison and multiplication equation to describe and model the problem.

_____ times as many as _____ is _____.

_____ × _____ = _____

D. Sasha unlocks _____ levels.

Turn and Talk Why can you use a multiplication equation to model this problem?

2 Landon wins 4 tickets for playing a car game. He wins 6 times as many tickets for the space game. How many tickets does Landon win for the space game?

A. Draw a bar model to represent the problem.

B. What equation can you use to model the problem?

_____

C. Interpret your equation as a comparison.

_____ is _____ times as many as _____.

D. Landon wins _____ tickets for the space game.

 Turn and Talk How do the bar model and equation represent each part of the comparison?

• •

Check Understanding

1 A superhero video game uses 6 coins. An airplane game uses twice as many coins as the superhero game. How many coins does the airplane game use? Complete the bar model, comparison, and equation to solve.

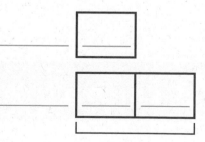

_____ times as many as _____ is _____.

_____ × _____ = _____

The airplane game uses _____ coins.

On Your Own

2 (MP) **Use Tools** Frank and Shari play basketball. Shari makes 2 baskets. Frank makes 4 times as many baskets as Shari. Complete the bar model and write an equation to find how many baskets Frank makes.

_____

(MP) **Model with Mathematics** Write a multiplication equation to model the comparison.

3 21 is 3 times as many as 7.

_____

4 8 times as many as 6 is 48.

_____

Interpret the multiplication equation as a comparison.

5 $45 = 9 \times 5$ _____

6 $4 \times 7 = 28$ _____

7 (MP) **Construct Arguments** Helen and Jamal write different equations to model the comparison *40 is 5 times as many as 8.* Who is correct? Explain.

_____

_____

Helen: $40 = 8 \times 5$

Jamal: $40 = 5 \times 8$

I'm in a Learning Mindset!

What tools can I use to represent multiplicative comparison problems?

_____

_____

Name _____

Distinguish Between Multiplicative and Additive Comparisons

(I Can) identify and represent multiplicative and additive comparison problems.

Spark Your Learning

Shanil makes a hexagon using 6 toothpicks. Rachel uses 2 more toothpicks than Shanil to make a shape. Leo uses 2 times as many toothpicks as Shanil to make a shape.

Use a visual model to show the number of toothpicks Shanil, Rachel, and Leo each use.

SMALL GROUPS

 Turn and Talk How is showing *2 more than 6* different from showing *2 times as many as 6*?

Build Understanding

1 Victor makes 4 paper cranes. Natalie makes 3 times as many cranes as Victor. How many paper cranes does Natalie make?

Use a visual model to represent the problem.

A. How can you use an equation to model the number of cranes Natalie makes? How many does she make?

_____

B. Suppose James makes 3 more cranes than Victor. What equation can you use to model the number of cranes James makes?

_____

C. How are the two equations different?

_____

_____

 Turn and Talk Which of your two equations models a multiplicative comparison problem? How do you know?

Step It Out

2 Maria makes a peacock with 8 feathers.
Simon uses 4 more feathers than Maria.
How many feathers does Simon use?

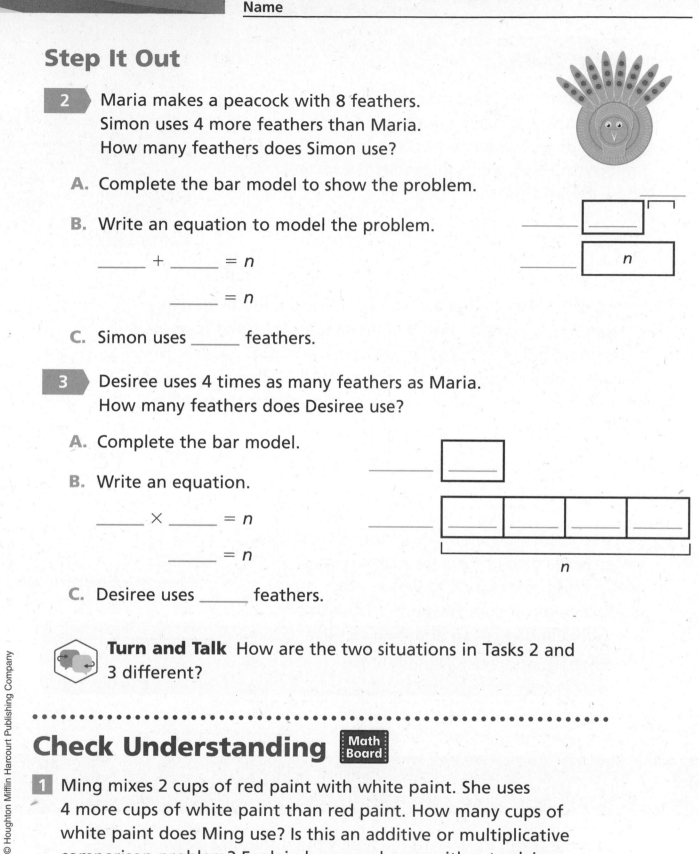

A. Complete the bar model to show the problem.

B. Write an equation to model the problem.

_____ + _____ = n

_____ = n

C. Simon uses _____ feathers.

3 Desiree uses 4 times as many feathers as Maria.
How many feathers does Desiree use?

A. Complete the bar model.

B. Write an equation.

_____ × _____ = n

_____ = n

C. Desiree uses _____ feathers.

Turn and Talk How are the two situations in Tasks 2 and 3 different?

Check Understanding Math Board

1 Ming mixes 2 cups of red paint with white paint. She uses 4 more cups of white paint than red paint. How many cups of white paint does Ming use? Is this an additive or multiplicative comparison problem? Explain how you know without solving.

_____

_____

On Your Own

2 (MP) **Reason** Cory makes these finger puppets. Jackie makes 6 times as many puppets as Cory. How many puppets does Jackie make? Is this an additive or multiplicative comparison problem? Explain how you know without solving.

_____

_____

3 (MP) **Model with Mathematics** Jen takes 6 minutes to make a paper animal. Brian takes 5 more minutes than Jen to make a paper animal. Kai takes 5 times as many minutes as Jen. How many minutes does it take Brian and Kai to each make a paper animal? Write an equation to model and solve each problem. Use *n* for the unknown.

Brian: _____

Kai: _____

4 (MP) **Use Tools** Hassan mixes 2 cups of water with oil to make a lava lamp. He uses 3 times as much oil as water. How many cups of oil does Hassan use? Use the bar model and write an equation to solve the problem. Use *c* for the unknown.

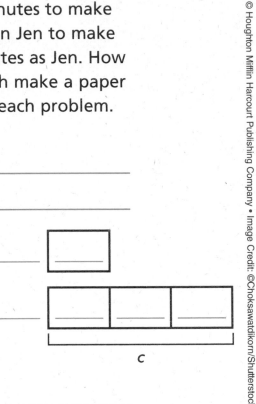

_____

_____

⬡ I'm in a Learning Mindset!

Is there anything still unclear to me about the difference between additive and multiplicative comparison problems? Explain.

_____

Name _____

Use Division to Solve Multiplicative Comparison Problems

(**I Can**) solve a multiplicative comparison problem by using division with drawings and equations.

Step It Out

1 ▸ Olivia is in the photography club. She takes 15 photos at a garden. That is 3 times as many photos as she takes at school. How many photos does Olivia take at school?

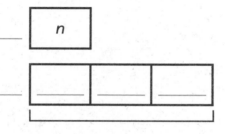

A. Use a bar model to show the problem. Let *n* represent the unknown.

B. Write an equation to model the problem. Use *n* for the unknown.

Problem: 3 times as many as *n* is 15.

Equation: _____ × *n* = _____

C. Use the inverse operation to solve the problem.

_____ ÷ _____ = *n*

_____ = *n*

> **Connect to Vocabulary**
>
> **Inverse operations,** such as multiplication and division, undo each other.
>
> 3 × 2 = 6
> 6 ÷ 3 = 2

D. Olivia takes _____ photos at school.

 **Turn and Talk** How did you represent *3 times as many* in your bar model and equations?

Step It Out

2 This year, 28 students are in the chess club. Last year, 7 students were in the club. How many times as many students are in the chess club this year than last year?

A. Write a multiplication equation to model the problem. Use *n* for the unknown.

$n \times \underline{\hspace{1.5cm}} = \underline{\hspace{1.5cm}}$

B. Write a division equation to solve the problem.

$\underline{\hspace{1.5cm}} \div \underline{\hspace{1.5cm}} = \underline{\hspace{1.5cm}}$

$\underline{\hspace{1.5cm}} = n$

This year, _____ times as many students are in the chess club.

Turn and Talk Why can you use division to solve a multiplicative comparison problem, but not an additive comparison problem?

Check Understanding [Math Board]

Write multiplication and division equations to model and solve the problem. Use *n* for the unknown.

1 Leslie collects 24 aluminum cans and 8 glass bottles for the recycling club. How many times as many cans as bottles does Leslie collect?

2 The students in the cooking club bake 12 blueberry muffins. They bake twice as many blueberry muffins as corn muffins. How many corn muffins do the students bake?

Leslie collects _____ times as many cans as bottles.

The students bake _____ corn muffins in the cooking club.

On Your Own

3 (MP) **Use Tools** The library club receives 56 fiction books and 8 nonfiction books. How many times as many fiction books as nonfiction books does the club receive?

Nonfiction	8

Fiction	8	8	8	8	8	8	8

56

_____

4 (MP) **Use Structure** Bob fills a basket with carnations and roses. He uses 18 roses and twice as many roses as carnations. How many carnations does Bob use?

• Write an equation to model the problem.

_____ ◯ $n =$ _____

• Use the inverse operation to write a different equation and solve the problem.

_____ ◯ _____ $= n$

_____

5 (MP) **Model with Mathematics** A sweater costs $40. That is 5 times as much as a shirt. What is the price of the shirt? Write multiplication and division equations to model and solve the problem. Use s for the unknown.

_____

_____

6 **Open Ended** Write a multiplicative comparison word problem that can be modeled and solved with the equations $7 \times m = 21$ and $21 \div 7 = m$.

_____

_____

On Your Own

7 (MP) **Use Tools** In the martial arts club, students spend 20 minutes working on blocking. That is 4 times as long as they spend meditating. How many minutes do the students spend meditating?

- Complete the bar model to show the problem.

- Use inverse operations to write equations to model and solve the problem.

_____ $\bigcirc$ _____ = _____

_____ $\bigcirc$ _____ = _____

_____

	m

_____

_____

8 Students in the engineering club build two train tracks. Track A is 24 feet long. That is 3 times as long as the length of Track B. What is the length of Track B? Show your work.

_____

9 (MP) **Critique Reasoning** Kevin walks 6 laps and jogs 2 laps. Kevin writes this equation to find how many times as many laps he walks as jogs. Is Kevin correct? Explain.

_____

_____

_____

$6 \times 2 = n$

$12 = n$

I walked 12 times as
many laps as I jogged.

© Houghton Mifflin Harcourt Publishing Company • Image Credit: ©Shutterstock

Name _____

Use Comparisons to Solve Problem Situations

(**I Can**) write equations with letters for the unknown values to model and solve multiplicative and additive comparison problems.

Step It Out

1 Anton is making chili for lunch at a soup kitchen. He uses 8 cups of navy beans. The recipe calls for 3 times as many black beans as navy beans. How many cups of black beans does Anton use?

A. Draw a box around what you want to know. Then underline the facts you will use.

B. Identify the type of comparison. _____

C. Identify the unknown in the comparison. Circle the answer.

smaller quantity   how many times as many

larger quantity   how many more/fewer

D. Write an equation to model the problem. Use *n* for the unknown.

smaller quantity + how many more/fewer = larger quantity
how many times as many × smaller quantity = larger quantity

_____

E. Solve the problem. Find the value for *n* that makes the

equation true. _____

F. Anton uses _____ cups of black beans.

 Turn and Talk How could you use a bar model or other visual model to represent the problem?

Step It Out

2 Some students are helping out at a soup kitchen. They bring in 42 cases of water and 7 cases of juice. How many more cases of water than juice do the students bring in?

A. Identify the type of comparison. _____

B. Identify the unknown. _____

C. Write an equation to model the comparison and solve the problem. Use *n* for the unknown.

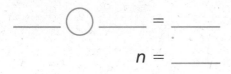

$$n = \underline{\quad}$$

D. The students bring in _____ more cases of water.

Turn and Talk Would you solve the problem differently if it asked how many times as many cases of water as juice? Explain.

Check Understanding `Math Board`

Write an equation to model and solve the problem.
Use *n* for the unknown.

1 Tina donates 3 fewer cans of corn than green beans. She donates 15 cans of green beans. How many cans of corn does Tina donate?

2 There are 42 students and 6 adults volunteering at the soup kitchen. How many times as many students as adults are volunteering?

Tina donates _____ cans of corn.

There are _____ times as many students as adults.

On Your Own

(MP) Model with Mathematics Write an equation to model and solve the problem. Use *n* for the unknown.

3 Mr. Torres makes 12 cups of rice and 8 cups of couscous for the soup kitchen. How many more cups of rice than couscous does Mr. Torres make?

_____

4 Carrie spends 45 minutes making chicken noodle soup. That is 5 times as many minutes as she spends making a salad. How many minutes does Carrie spend making the salad?

_____

5 **(MP) Reason** Draw a line to match each comparison problem to the equation that models it.

- Sam has 18 cards. That is 3 times as many cards as Lena has. How many cards does Lena have? •

- Lena has 6 cards. Sam has 18 cards. How many more cards does Sam have than Lena? •

- Sam has 12 more cards than Lena. Lena has 6 cards. How many cards does Sam have? •

- Lena has 6 cards. Sam has 3 times as many cards as Lena. How many cards does Sam have? •

- Sam has 12 more cards than Lena. Sam has 18 cards. How many cards does Lena have? •

- Sam has 18 cards. Lena has 6 cards. How many times as many cards does Sam have as Lena? •

• $n + 12 = 18$

• $3 \times 6 = n$

• $6 + n = 18$

• $6 + 12 = n$

• $n \times 6 = 18$

• $3 \times n = 18$

On Your Own

6 (MP) **Use Structure** Ms. Novak volunteers 15 hours at the soup kitchen this week. That is 5 times as many hours as Gina volunteers. How many hours does Gina volunteer at the soup kitchen?

Use inverse operations to write two different equations to model the problem. Let h = the number of hours Gina volunteers.

_____ ◯ _____ = _____   _____ ◯ _____ = _____

$h =$ _____   _____ $= h$

_____

(MP) **Model with Mathematics** Write an equation to model and solve the problem. Use n for the unknown.

7 Joshua makes these centerpieces. He makes 2 fewer centerpieces than Betty. How many centerpieces does Betty make?

_____

8 Five students sign up to be cooks at the soup kitchen.

- Four more students sign up to be servers than cooks. How many students sign up to be servers?

_____

- Four times as many students sign up to be cleaners as cooks. How many students sign up to be cleaners?

_____

Name _____

Solve Multistep Problems with Multiplication and Division

(I Can) solve multistep problems with multiplication and division by writing equations with letters representing the unknown quantities.

Step It Out

1 ▶ Airboats are a popular way to tour areas with shallow water. A small airboat can fit 6 people. A large airboat can fit 4 times as many people. How many more people can fit in a large airboat than in a small airboat?

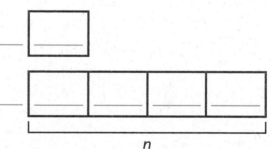

Break up the problem into smaller steps. Use a bar model and equation to complete each step.

A. Find how many people fit in a large airboat, *n*.

_____ × _____ = n

_____ = n

_____ people can fit in a large airboat.

B. Use the result from Part A to find how many more people fit in a large airboat, *m*.

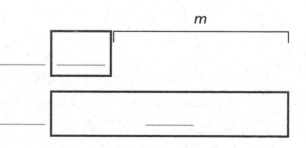

_____ + m = _____

m = _____

_____ more people can fit in a large airboat.

 Turn and Talk Could you have done the steps in a different order to solve the problem? Explain.

Step It Out

2 ▶ A park has reptile shows every weekend. There were 27 people at the show on Saturday. That is 3 times as many people as on Sunday. How many people saw the show that weekend?

Write an equation for each step.

A. Find how many people saw the show on Sunday, s.

_____ people saw the show on Sunday.

$$\_\_\_\_ \times s = \_\_\_\_$$

$$\_\_\_\_ \div \_\_\_\_ = s$$

$$\_\_\_\_ = s$$

B. Use the result from Part A to find how many people saw the show that weekend, w.

That weekend, _____ people saw the show.

$$\_\_\_\_ + \_\_\_\_ = w$$

$$\_\_\_\_ = w$$

 Turn and Talk How could you use pictures or bar models to help solve the problem?

• •

Check Understanding `Math Board`

Write equations to model and solve the problem. Use letters for the unknowns.

1 Mette counts 5 birds and 8 times as many insects in a park. How many more insects than birds does Mette count?

2 There are 7 times as many toys as maps in the gift shop. There are 35 toys. How many toys and maps are in the gift shop?

She counts _____ more insects.

_____ toys and maps are in the shop.

© Houghton Mifflin Harcourt Publishing Company • Image Credit: ©Ameng Wu/iStockphoto.com/Getty Images

On Your Own

3 (MP) **Use Tools** Students in the third and fourth grades plant trees in a park. The third graders plant 7 trees. The fourth graders plant 3 times as many trees. How many trees do students in the two grades plant? Use a visual model or an equation to complete each step.

- Find the number of trees the fourth graders plant, *m*.

- Find the number of trees students in the two grades plant, *n*.

4 (MP) **Model with Mathematics** Aditi takes 72 photos of animals. That is 9 times as many photos as Shane takes. How many fewer photos does Shane take than Aditi?

Write equations to model and solve the problem. Let *s* = the number of photos Shane takes. Let *f* = how many fewer photos Shane takes than Aditi.

On Your Own

(MP) Model with Mathematics Write equations to model and solve the problem. Use letters for the unknowns.

5 Rebecca sees 5 manatees swimming in Florida's Crystal River. Maya sees 3 times as many manatees as Rebecca. How many more manatees does Maya see than Rebecca?

_____

6 Geography Nevada is the driest state. In most years, it gets only 9 inches of rain. Florida usually gets 6 times as much rain as Nevada. The rainiest state, Hawaii, usually gets 10 more inches of rain than Florida each year. About how many inches of rain does Hawaii get in most years?

_____

7 STEM Bromeliads are plants that are adapted to different climates. The leaf bases of some bromeliads catch and hold water. This helps the plant survive in dry conditions. A scientist measures the water held in two bromeliads. The first has 3 fluid ounces. The second has twice as much water as the first. How much water do the two bromeliads hold?

_____

8 Open Ended Write a multistep word problem than can be modeled by these equations.

$4 \times n = 24$
$n = 6$
$24 + 6 = t$
$30 = t$

_____

Name _____

Review

Vocabulary

1 Draw a visual model and write a pair of equations to show why multiplication and division are inverse operations.

_____

Concepts and Skills

2 How can you interpret the meaning of the equation $30 = 3 \times 10$ as a comparison?

Ⓐ 30 is 3 more than 10.   Ⓒ 10 is 3 times a many as 30.

Ⓑ 10 is 3 fewer than 30.   Ⓓ 30 is 3 times as many as 10.

3 Diane waits 6 minutes in line to buy movie tickets. Josh waits in line 4 times as long as Diane. Let m = the number of minutes Josh waits in line. Select all the equations that can be used to find m.

Ⓐ $6 + 4 = m$ Ⓒ $6 - 4 = m$ Ⓔ $4 + 6 = m$

Ⓑ $6 \times 4 = m$ Ⓓ $4 + 4 + 4 + 4 = m$ Ⓕ $4 \times 6 = m$

4 ⓂⓅ **Use Tools** Jake has 40 pencils. That is 8 times as many as the pens he has. How many pens does Jake have? Tell what strategy or tool you will use to answer the question, explain your choice, and then find the answer.

Ⓐ 5   Ⓑ 8   Ⓒ 32   Ⓓ 48

_____

Write equations to model and solve the problem. Use letters for the unknowns.

5 Alisha takes 7 minutes to solve a puzzle. Riley takes 4 more minutes than Alisha to solve the puzzle. Jordan takes 3 times as many minutes as Alisha to solve the puzzle. How long does it take Riley and Jordan to each solve the puzzle?

Riley: _____

Jordan: _____

6 Mei has 18 red marbles. That is 3 times as many as the number of yellow marbles she has. She has 10 fewer green marbles than red marbles. How many green marbles does Mei have? How many yellow?

Green: _____

Yellow: _____

7 During this year's park survey, rangers counted 28 eagles. That is 4 times as many as they counted in last year's survey. How many more eagles did the rangers count this year than last year?

_____

8 Mr. Carney tells his class to draw pictures of different types of birds for the class bulletin board. Joel draws 8 pictures. Taylor draws 3 times as many pictures as Joel. If 4 pictures can fit in a row, how many rows of the board can Taylor fill?

_____

Mental Math and Estimation Strategies

How large is the room?

- The adoption room at a local animal shelter has four visiting spaces.

- Two of the four visiting spaces have tiled floors. Each tile has an area of 4 square feet.

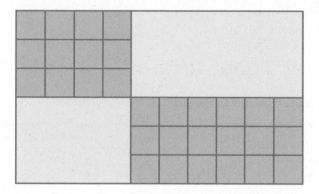

- What is the area of the adoption room?

_____

 **Turn and Talk**

- What strategy did you use to find the area? Explain each step.

- The manager of the animal shelter wants to separate the adoption room into 3 equal sections for an event. How can you find the area of each section?

Are You Ready?

Complete these problems to review prior concepts and skills you will need for this module.

Multiplication and Division Related Facts

Write the related facts for the array.

1 _____ × _____ = _____

_____ × _____ = _____

_____ ÷ _____ = _____

_____ ÷ _____ = _____

Meaning of Division: Equal Groups

Complete the table. Use counters to help.

	Counters	Number of Equal Groups	Number in Each Group
2	15	3	
3	20		2
4	6		3
5	12	3	
6	24		6
7	42	6	
8	72	8	

Unknown Factors

Find the unknown factor.

9 8 × _____ = 40   **10** _____ × 9 = 36   **11** 8 = _____ × 4

12 35 = 5 × _____   **13** 7 × _____ = 21   **14** 4 × _____ = 16

Name _____

Explore Multiplication Patterns with Tens, Hundreds, and Thousands

(I Can) use basic facts, patterns, and place value to multiply a multiple of 10, 100, or 1,000 by a 1-digit number.

COME AND SEE THE PLAY!
TICKETS
$100
EACH

Spark Your Learning

Tickets to the play just went on sale. Charles wants to buy 5 tickets. How much does he spend?

Show your thinking.

SMALL GROUPS

Turn and Talk What basic multiplication facts can help you solve the problem? Why do they help?

Build Understanding

1 There are 8 bags of pencil-top erasers for the school store. How many erasers are there if each bag has 70 erasers? 700 erasers?

Start with a simpler number. Represent how many erasers there are if each bag contains 7 erasers. Write a multiplication equation for the basic fact you show.

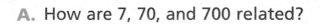

A. How are 7, 70, and 700 related?

_____

B. How can you use the renamed numbers and basic facts to find each product?

$8 \times 7 =$ _____

$8 \times 70 = 8 \times$ _____ tens = _____ tens = _____

$8 \times 700 = 8 \times$ _____ hundreds = _____ hundreds = _____

There will be _____ erasers if each bag has 70 erasers and _____ erasers if each bag has 700 erasers.

 Turn and Talk How can you use place value and basic facts to find how many erasers there are if each bag has 7,000 erasers?

2 In a game at the school fair, each player tries to throw 3 balls into these baskets. Each basket scores different points. What will be a player's total score if all 3 balls land in the same basket?

A. Complete the equations to model all the possible total scores.

$3 \times 1 =$ _____ points ⟵ basic fact

$3 \times 10 =$ _____ points

$3 \times 100 =$ _____ points

$3 \times 1,000 =$ _____ points

B. What is the same about all the equations?

_____

C. What patterns do you see in the equations?

_____

Turn and Talk Which equation shows 3×10 tens $= 30$ tens? How do you know?

Check Understanding Math Board

1 One game gives 1,000 points for a win. How many points are earned after 4 wins?

$4 \times 1 = 4$

$4 \times 10 = 40$

$4 \times 100 =$ _____

$4 \times 1,000 =$ _____

_____ points are earned.

2 Each box has 8 prizes. How many prizes are in 5,000 boxes?

$5 \times 8 = 40$

$50 \times 8 = 400$

$500 \times 8 =$ _____

$5,000 \times 8 =$ _____

There are _____ prizes.

© Houghton Mifflin Harcourt Publishing Company

On Your Own

3 (MP) **Use Structure** The fourth grade class is selling pencils for a school fundraiser. The pencils come in boxes of 4,000 pencils. If 5 boxes of pencils are sold, how many pencils did the fourth grade class sell?

5×4 ones = _____ ones

$5 \times 4 =$ _____

5×4 tens = _____ tens

$5 \times 40 =$ _____

5×4 hundreds = _____ hundreds

$5 \times 400 =$ _____

5×4 thousands = _____ thousands

$5 \times 4,000 =$ _____

The fourth grade class sells _____ pencils.

4 Jeremy writes some notes about patterns when multiplying with tens, hundreds, and thousands. Fill in the blanks to complete his notes.

5 The school uses the money they raised to buy 3 new basketball hoops. Each hoop costs $600. What is the cost for the 3 hoops?

_____

7×30 is the same as $7 \times$ _____ tens.

9×200 is the same as $9 \times$ _____ hundreds.

$2 \times 5,000$ is the same as $2 \times$ _____ thousands.

$6 \times 7,000$ is the same as $6 \times$ _____ thousands.

6 Use place value and patterns to find the products.

$4 \times 300 =$ _____ $9 \times 8,000 =$ _____

➗ I'm in a Learning Mindset!

What do I already know that can help me multiply with tens, hundreds, and thousands on my own?

_____

_____

© Houghton Mifflin Harcourt Publishing Company

Name _____

Explore Division Patterns with Tens, Hundreds, and Thousands

(I Can) use basic facts, patterns, and place value to divide a multiple of 10, 100, or 1,000 by a 1-digit number.

Spark Your Learning

The Golden Gate Bridge is a famous landmark in California. A toy store has a model on display of the bridge made out of blocks. The model is made using 9,000 blocks. Before it is put together, the blocks are stored in 3 bins. Each bin has the same number of blocks.

How many blocks are in each bin?

Show your thinking.

SMALL GROUPS

Turn and Talk What basic facts can help you solve the problem? Why do they help?

Build Understanding

1 The toy store sells toy cars in packs of 320. A group of 8 friends wants to share one pack. How many toy cars will each friend get?

Start with a simpler number. Represent how many cars each friend would get from a pack of 32 cars. Write a division equation for the basic fact you show.

A. How are 32 and 320 related?

_____

B. How can you use the simpler numbers along with place value and basic facts to find the answer?

_____

_____

 Turn and Talk How could you use base-ten blocks to show 320 ÷ 8?

Name _____

Step It Out

2 The toy store sells sticker sets for $9. How many sets does the store have to sell to make $270? $2,700?

    A. Use place value to rename the numbers.

        270 = _____ tens

        2,700 = _____ hundreds

    B. Use a basic fact and the renamed numbers to find each quotient.

        $27 \div 9 =$ _____   ⟵ basic fact

        $270 \div 9 =$ _____ tens ÷ 9 = _____ tens = _____

        $2,700 \div 9 =$ _____ hundreds ÷ 9 = _____ hundreds = _____

        The store needs to sell _____ sets to make $270 and _____ sets to make $2,700.

     Turn and Talk What patterns do you see in the three division equations?

Check Understanding   Math Board

1 Two friends split a $2,000 prize. How much money do they each get?

$2 \div 2 = 1$

$20 \div 2 = 10$

$200 \div 2 =$ _____

$2,000 \div 2 =$ _____

They each get _____.

2 Ari has 2,000 marbles. He puts the same number of marbles in each of 5 bags. How many marbles are in each bag?

$20 \div 5 = 4$

$200 \div 5 = 40$

$2,000 \div 5 =$ _____

_____ marbles are in each bag.

On Your Own

3 (MP) **Use Structure** A printer needs to send 3,000 books to 6 libraries. Each library must get the same number of books. How many books should the printer send to each library? Complete the pattern to solve.

30 ÷ 6 = 5

300 ÷ 6 = 50

3,000 ÷ 6 = _____

The printer should send _____ books to each library.

4 A dairy farm produces 8,000 gallons of milk each week. The milk is stored in these tanks. Each tank holds the same amount of milk. How many gallons

does 1 tank hold? _____

5 Use place value and patterns to find the quotients.

630 ÷ 7 = _____   4,500 ÷ 9 = _____

6 **Open Ended** Write and solve a word problem that can be modeled and solved with the equation 2,800 ÷ 4 = ■.

_____

_____

_____

🎲 I'm in a Learning Mindset!

Is there anything still unclear to me about dividing tens, hundreds, and thousands? Explain.

_____

Name _____

Estimate Products by 1-Digit Numbers

(I Can) estimate products of 1-digit numbers and determine whether the exact product is reasonable.

Spark Your Learning

Emma works for a traveling carnival. She needs to order 84 stuffed prizes for each of the 6 game booths. Emma estimates that she needs to order about 480 prizes. Is her estimate reasonable?

Show your thinking.

Turn and Talk How did you change the numbers in the problem to estimate? Why?

Build Understanding

1 The roller coaster at the carnival runs for 6 hours every day. It can take 320 people for a ride each hour. About how many people can go on the roller coaster each day?

Use a visual model to show how you can estimate the product 6 × 320.

A. How did you change the numbers to estimate?

_____

B. What two estimates do you get for 6 × 320 when you round 320 to the two nearest hundreds?

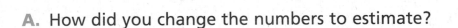

_____ × _____ = _____

_____ × _____ = _____

C. Which estimate is more reasonable? Why?

_____

_____

About _____ people can go on the roller coaster each day.

Turn and Talk How is finding an estimate different from finding an exact answer?

Name _____

Step It Out

2 ▶ The first Ferris wheel could carry
2,160 passengers per rotation. Suppose
4 groups rode the Ferris wheel with every
seat filled each time. Emma says that
8,640 people rode the Ferris wheel. Is Emma's
statement reasonable? Estimate 4 × 2,160.

A. Identify the two thousands that 2,160 is
between. Circle them on the number line.

```
◄──┬──┬──┬──┬──┬──┬──┬──┬──┬──┬──┬──┬──┬──┬──┬──┬──┬──┬──┬──┬──►
  1,000        1,500        2,000        2,500        3,000
```

B. Use those two thousands to estimate two products that
the exact product is between.

$4 \times 2{,}160$ $\qquad\qquad$ $4 \times 2{,}160$

$\downarrow$ $\qquad\qquad\qquad$ $\downarrow$

$4 \times$ _____ = _____ $\qquad$ $4 \times$ _____ = _____

The product $4 \times 2{,}160$ is between _____ and _____.

Emma's estimate of 8,640 is _____.

🗨 **Turn and Talk** How do your estimates show whether or not
Emma's exact answer is reasonable?

• •

Check Understanding [Math Board]

1 Tickets to the carnival cost $7. The cashier sells 225 tickets in one
hour. She says that the ticket sales in that hour were $950. Is this
reasonable? Use estimation to justify your answer.

_____

_____

2 Use rounding to estimate $4 \times 3{,}122$. _____

© Houghton Mifflin Harcourt Publishing Company • Image Credit: ©Alphonse Leong/Shutterstock

Module 4 • Lesson 3

87

On Your Own

(MP) **Construct Arguments** Determine if the answer is reasonable. Explain.

3 Greta has 3 rolls of ride tickets for the carnival. Each roll has 64 tickets. She says that she has 192 tickets.

_____

_____

4 Mr. Thomas sells these sun visors at the carnival. He sells 415 sun visors in one month. Mr. Thomas says that his monthly sales were $3,320.

_____

_____

$8

Use rounding to estimate the product.

5 6×479

6 3×92

7 $8 \times 1,659$

_____   _____   _____

Find two estimates that the product is between.

8 $9 \times 3,217$

The product is between

_____ and _____ .

9 7×624

The product is between

_____ and _____ .

© Houghton Mifflin Harcourt Publishing Company

➗ I'm in a Learning Mindset!

What questions can I ask my teacher or classmates to help me understand how to estimate products?

_____

_____

Name

Estimate Quotients Using Compatible Numbers

(I Can) estimate the quotient of a division problem involving a 1-digit divisor using compatible numbers.

Spark Your Learning

Myra has a part-time job as a lifeguard at Lazy Daze Summer Camp. She works 78 hours over 4 weeks. Myra estimates how many hours she works each week.

$80 \div 4 = 20$

Myra says she works about 20 hours each week.

Do you agree? Show your thinking.

 Turn and Talk How did Myra change the numbers in the problem to estimate?

Build Understanding

1 Lazy Daze Summer Camp will host 624 campers during 3 sessions. About how many campers will attend each session?

Show how you can estimate the quotient 624 ÷ 3.

A. Circle a number on the number line that is close to 624 that is easier to divide by 3.

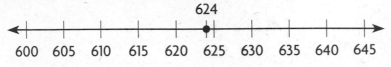

624

600 605 610 615 620 625 630 635 640 645

B. How can you use basic facts to find compatible numbers for dividing 624 by 3?

_____ ÷ 3 = 1, so 300 divides easily by 3.

_____ ÷ 3 = 2, so 600 divides easily by 3.

_____ ÷ 3 = 3, so 900 divides easily by 3.

_____ ÷ 3 = 4, so 1,200 divides easily by 3.

> **Connect to Vocabulary**
>
> **Compatible numbers** are numbers that are easy to compute mentally and are close to the exact numbers in the problem.

C. Which compatible number for 3 will you use? Explain.

_____

D. Choose the compatible number for 3 that is closest to 624. How can you use a basic fact and place value to divide your chosen compatible numbers?

_____

_____

About _____ campers will attend each session.

 Turn and Talk How do you know that your estimate for the quotient 624 ÷ 3 is reasonable?

Step It Out

2 ▸ Shannon has 1,880 energy bars to make welcome packets for campers. She puts 4 energy bars in each packet. Shannon says that she can make 470 welcome packets. Is this reasonable?

Estimate 1,880 ÷ 4.

A. Find two compatible numbers for 4 that 1,880 is between.

16 ÷ 4 = 4, so _____ divides easily by 4.

20 ÷ 4 = 5, so _____ divides easily by 4.

B. Use those two numbers to estimate two quotients that the exact quotient is between.

1,880 ÷ 4   1,880 ÷ 4
    ↓   ↓
_____ ÷ 4 = _____   _____ ÷ 4 = _____

The quotient 1,880 ÷ 4 is between _____ and _____.

Turn and Talk How do your estimates show that Shannon's exact answer is reasonable?

Check Understanding

1 Lazy Daze Summer Camp has tents that each fit 5 campers. The camp director says they need 78 tents for 290 campers. Is this reasonable? Use estimation to justify your answer.

_____

_____

2 Use compatible numbers to estimate the quotient.

1,765 ÷ 6 _____

On Your Own

MP Construct Arguments Determine if the answer is reasonable. Explain.

3 Jenna marks her calendar to show how many days until summer camp starts. Jenna says that the camp starts in 13 weeks.

_____

_____

_____

March calendar showing 147 days until Summer Camp! with the 7th circled.

4 Each flashlight costs $8. The director of Lazy Daze Camp says that $4,480 will buy enough flashlights for 560 campers.

_____

_____

Use compatible numbers to estimate the quotient.

5 33 ÷ 3

6 352 ÷ 7

7 8,214 ÷ 9

_____

_____

_____

Find two estimates that the quotient is between.

8 510 ÷ 6

The quotient is between

_____ and _____.

9 2,945 ÷ 4

The quotient is between

_____ and _____.

⚙ I'm in a Learning Mindset!

How do I help my partner understand using compatible numbers to estimate quotients?

_____

Name _____

Use Mental Math Strategies for Multiplication and Division

(I Can) use properties of operations and the relationship between multiplication and division to find products and quotients using mental math.

Step It Out

1 James crochets a pattern with this yarn. Each color has 7 rows with 50 stitches in each row. How many stitches are in the pattern?

Find $4 \times 7 \times 50$.

A. Use the Commutative Property.

$4 \times 7 \times 50 = 4 \times$ _____ $\times 7$

B. Use basic facts and place value to multiply two factors.

Think: $4 \times 5 = 20$, so $4 \times 50 =$ _____.

C. Multiply the result by the third factor.

$4 \times 50 \times 7 =$ _____ $\times 7 =$ _____

There are _____ stitches in the pattern.

> **Connect to Vocabulary**
>
> The **Commutative Property of Multiplication** states that when the order of the factors is changed, the product is the same.

2 Find $325 \div 5$.

A. Use addition. Break the dividend into two parts that divide easily by 5.

$325 \div 5 = ($ _____ $+$ _____ $) \div 5$

B. Divide each part and then add the two quotients.

$325 \div 5 = (300 \div 5) + (25 \div 5)$

$= $ _____ $+$ _____ $=$ _____

Step It Out

 3 Mei has 800 craft sticks for 4 projects. How many craft sticks can she use for each project?

Find 800 ÷ 4.

A. Use the relationship between multiplication and division.

> **Think:** What number when multiplied by _____ equals 800?

B. Use basic facts and place value to solve.

> **Think:** $4 \times 2 = 8$, so $4 \times$ _____ $= 800$.

800 ÷ 4 = _____

Each project can use _____ craft sticks.

4 Find 5×72.

A. Use place value to rewrite the equation.

$5 \times 72 = 5 \times ($ _____ $+$ _____ $)$

B. Use the Distributive Property and solve.

$5 \times 72 = (5 \times$ _____ $) + (5 \times$ _____ $)$

$= $ _____ $+$ _____

$= $ _____

> **Connect to Vocabulary**
>
> The **Distributive Property** states that multiplying a sum by a number is the same as multiplying each addend by the number and then adding the products.

 Turn and Talk What other strategies can you use to multiply and divide with mental math?

Check Understanding 🔲 Math Board

Use mental math to find the product or the quotient.

1 $30 \times 8 \times 2 = $ _____   **2** $450 \div 5 = $ _____

On Your Own

Use mental math to find the product or the quotient. Tell which strategy you used.

3 $20 \times 9 \times 5$

_____

_____

4 $8,800 \div 8$

_____

_____

5 $342 \div 6$

_____

_____

6 7×48

_____

_____

7 Melissa works at a pet store that sells aquarium fish. She puts 120 fish into 4 different tanks. Melissa puts the same number of fish in each tank. How many fish are in each tank?

Find $120 \div 4$.

_____

8 Jordan makes 4 beaded necklaces. Each necklace has 36 beads. How many beads does Jordan use to make the necklaces?

Find 4×36.

_____

On Your Own

Use mental math to find the product or the quotient. Tell which strategy you used.

9 James and Michael each buy 6 of these packages of small toy dinosaurs. How many toy dinosaurs do James and Michael buy?

Find $2 \times 6 \times 15$.

_____

10 A scientist counts 1,600 birds in an area covering 8 square miles of rainforest. About how many birds are in each square mile?

Find $1,600 \div 8$.

_____

11 **STEM** On a cold night, a hummingbird will go into a sleep-like state to save energy. In this state, the bird's heart rate can slow to around 55 beats per minute. If a hummingbird is in this sleep-like state for 8 minutes, how many times will it's heart beat?

Find 8×55.

_____

12 **Open Ended** Alan uses halving and doubling to find $240 \div 6$. What is another way he could find the quotient?

_____

_____

$$240 \div 6 = \blacksquare$$
$$240 \div 2 = 120$$
$$120 \div 6 = 20$$
$$2 \times 20 = 40$$
$$240 \div 6 = 40$$

Module 4 Review

Vocabulary

Choose the correct term from the Vocabulary box to complete the sentence.

Vocabulary
Commutative Property
compatible numbers
Distributive Property
place value

1 Numbers that are easy to use for mental computation are called _____.

2 The _____ states that multiplying a sum by a number is the same as multiplying each addend by the number and then adding the products.

3 The _____ of Multiplication states that when the order of the factors is changed, the product in the same.

Concepts and Skills

(MP) **Use Tools** Complete the pattern. Name the strategy or tool you will use to solve the problem, explain your choice, and then find the answer.

4 $6 \times 5 =$ _____

$6 \times 50 =$ _____

$6 \times 500 =$ _____

$6 \times 5,000 =$ _____

5 $56 \div 8 =$ _____

$560 \div 8 =$ _____

$5,600 \div 8 =$ _____

_____

_____

Use place value and patterns to find the product or the quotient.

6 $7 \times 300 =$ _____

7 $2,400 \div 6 =$ _____

Estimate the product.

8 4 × 3,189 _____

9 8 × 591 _____

10 3 × 627 _____

Estimate the quotient.

11 348 ÷ 7 _____

12 1,812 ÷ 3 _____

13 8,209 ÷ 9 _____

14 Select all the equations that have a value of 200.

   Ⓐ 5 × 40 = ▪

   Ⓑ 120 ÷ 6 = ▪

   Ⓒ 2 × 5 × 100 = ▪

   Ⓓ 10 × 2 × 10 = ▪

   Ⓔ 8,000 ÷ 4 = ▪

   Ⓕ 1,800 ÷ 9 = ▪

Use mental math to find the product or quotient.

15 20 × 8 × 5 _____

16 420 ÷ 6 _____

17 5 × 36 _____

18 Tickets to the carnival cost $7. The manager sells 225 tickets in one hour. Which of the following best estimates the ticket sales for that hour?

   Ⓐ It is between $200 and $300.

   Ⓑ It is between $700 and $1,400.

   Ⓒ It is between $1,400 and $2,100.

   Ⓓ It is between $2,100 and $2,800.

19 Paul sells glow sticks at the fair. Each glow stick costs $3. He sells 184 glow sticks in one week. Paul says that his weekly sales are $552. Is this reasonable? Why or why not?

_____

_____

5 Multiply by 1-Digit Numbers

How can YOU and your friends spend the least?

- You and 7 friends want to enter an amusement park. The park has the group rates shown on the sign.

ADMISSION PRICES
Single Ticket $70

GROUP TICKETS

2 tickets for $60 each
3 tickets for $50 each
4 tickets for $40 each
5 tickets for $30 each

- How much would it cost if you and your 7 friends all buy single tickets?

_____

- How can you and your friends all buy tickets and spend the least amount of money?

_____

 Turn and Talk

- How did you find the answer?

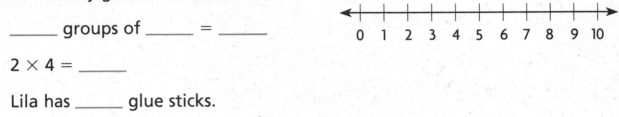

Are You Ready?

Complete these problems to review prior concepts and skills you will need for this module.

Practice Multiplication Facts

Use a number line to find the product.

1 Lila has 2 boxes of glue sticks. Each box has 4 glue sticks.

How many glue sticks does Lila have?

_____ groups of _____ = _____

$2 \times 4 =$ _____

Lila has _____ glue sticks.

0 1 2 3 4 5 6 7 8 9 10

Multiplication Facts

Find the product.

2 6×3

_____

3 2×7

_____

4 8×5

_____

5 3×8

_____

6 9×3

_____

7 5×5

_____

Multiples of 10, 100, and 1,000

Find the product.

8 $2 \times 1 =$ _____

$2 \times 10 =$ _____

$2 \times 100 =$ _____

$2 \times 1,000 =$ _____

9 $4 \times 8 =$ _____

$4 \times 80 =$ _____

$4 \times 800 =$ _____

$4 \times 8,000 =$ _____

10 $6 \times 7 =$ _____

$6 \times 70 =$ _____

$6 \times 700 =$ _____

$6 \times 7,000 =$ _____

Name

Represent Multiplication

(I Can) describe how to represent multiplication using arrays or
concrete models such as counters and base-ten blocks.

Spark Your Learning

A pint contains 24 strawberries. How can you show
the number of strawberries in 3 pints?

Draw a visual model to represent the problem.

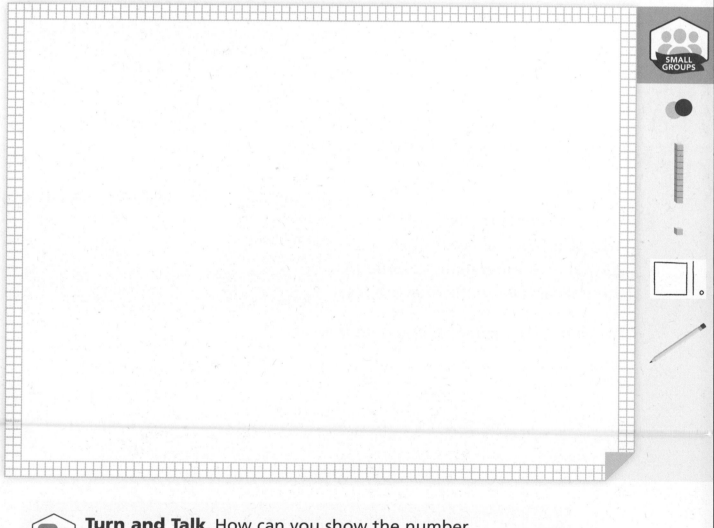

Turn and Talk How can you show the number
of strawberries in 3 pints another way?

Build Understanding

1 A standard apple tree can grow 13 bushels of apples. How can you use base-ten blocks to show the number of bushels 2 standard apple trees can grow?

Draw a quick picture to show your work.

Turn and Talk How can you write an equation to represent the number of bushels 2 standard apple trees can grow?

2 The guacamole recipe uses avocados. Each avocado has 234 calories. How many calories in the guacamole are from avocados?

GUACAMOLE RECIPE	
3 avocados	$\frac{1}{2}$ medium onion
1 lime, juiced	$\frac{1}{2}$ jalapeno
$\frac{1}{2}$ teaspoon salt	2 Roma tomatoes
$\frac{1}{2}$ teaspoon ground cumin	1 tablespoon cilantro
$\frac{1}{2}$ teaspoon cayenne	1 clove garlic

Draw a quick picture to show your work.

A. How can you use place value and base-ten blocks to find the number of calories in 3 avocados?

_____

_____

B. How can you write a multiplication equation for the base-ten block representation?

_____

_____

_____

 Turn and Talk How can you use place value and base-ten blocks to find the number of calories in 4 avocados?

• •

Check Understanding 🟦 Math Board

1 There are 126 apples in a bushel. How can you use base-ten blocks to show the number of apples in 4 bushels?

_____

2 Use base-ten blocks to show 6 × 13. Draw a quick picture to show your work.

3 Write a multiplication equation for the representation.

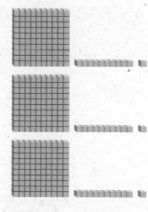

_____

On Your Own

4 (MP) **Reason** A pumpkin patch has 6 rows with 45 pumpkins in each row. How can you use base-ten blocks to show how many pumpkins are in the pumpkin patch?

_____

_____

Use base-ten blocks to show the product. Draw a quick picture to show your work.

5 3 × 214

6 2 × 32

7 Four watermelons each weigh 22 pounds. Use base-ten blocks to show how much the watermelons weigh. Draw a quick picture to show your work.

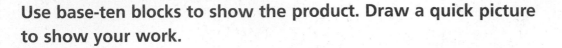

🔶 I'm in a Learning Mindset!

How did practice with base ten blocks help me master representing multiplication?

_____

_____

© Houghton Mifflin Harcourt Publishing Company • Image Credit: ©Getty Images

Name _____

Use Area Models and the Distributive Property to Multiply

(I Can) break apart a 2-digit factor to multiply a 2-digit factor by a 1-digit factor.

Spark Your Learning

A school scramble band gets into formation for a parade. There are 9 rows of 18 band members. How can you make a visual model to show the number of band members that are in the scramble band?

Draw a quick picture to show your work.

SMALL GROUPS

There are _____ band members in the scramble band.

Turn and Talk Why is this a good visual model for the problem?

Build Understanding

1 Willow is working through some math homework.
She comes to $7 \times 13 = \blacksquare$. How can she use an area model
to help her find the product?

A. How can you draw a rectangle on the grid to
show 7×13?

_____

_____

**Draw and label the rectangle as a combination of two
smaller rectangles.**

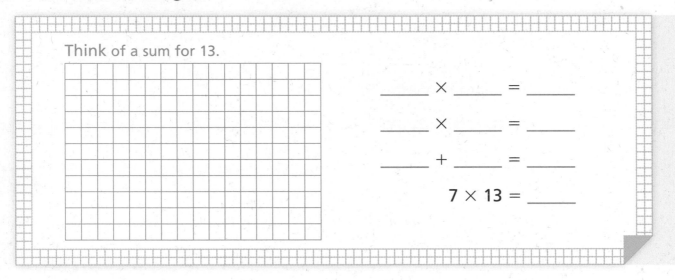

Think of a sum for 13.

_____ × _____ = _____

_____ × _____ = _____

_____ + _____ = _____

$7 \times 13 =$ _____

B. How can you use the *Distributive Property* and the area
model to make multiplying easier?

_____

_____

C. How can you find the product?

_____

_____

 Turn and Talk How can you represent 7×13 again,
thinking of a different sum for 13?

2 The next problem on Willow's homework sheet is 3 × 19 = ▪. How can you use base-ten blocks to show 3 × 19?

Draw a quick picture to show your work.

A. How can you use the Distributive Property to break apart the base-ten blocks and find the product?

_____

B. Draw a circle around the tens and a circle around the ones. Then write the numbers to solve.

(_____ × _____ ten) + (_____ × _____ ones)

(_____ × _____) + (_____ × _____)

_____ + _____

3 × 19 = _____

• •

Check Understanding `Math Board`

1 Find the product.

4 × 14 = _____

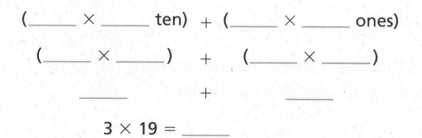

2 Draw an area model to represent the product.

3 × 11 = _____

On Your Own

3 How can you use an area model to show the product?

8 × 18 = _____

_____

_____

_____

_____

4 Draw an area model to represent the product.

5 × 14 = _____

5 Find the product.

7 × 16 = _____

6 (MP) **Reason** Why does the Distributive Property make it easier to multiply a 2-digit number by a 1-digit number?

_____

_____

_____

🔲 I'm in a Learning Mindset!

Was I able to finish my work? What helps me stay on task?

_____

_____

Name _____

Multiply Using Expanded Form

(I Can) use partial products to find the product of a 1-digit number and a 3-digit number.

Spark Your Learning

A community theater seats 123 people. A new play will run 4 shows. All of the seats are sold for all of the shows. How many tickets were sold?

SMALL GROUPS

_____ tickets sold for 4 shows.

Turn and Talk How can you solve the problem another way?

Build Understanding

1 To build the sets for the play, the stage crew manager buys 3 boxes of nails with 115 nails in each box. How many nails does he buy?

A. How can you write 115 in expanded form?

_____

B. How can you use the Distributive Property to find the number of nails the stage manager buys?

_____

Draw an area model using expanded form to help you find the product. Then use the Distributive Property to record the product for each smaller rectangle.

_____ × _____ = _____

_____ × _____ = _____

_____ × _____ = _____

Each part shows a partial product and is part of the whole product.

C. How can you use the partial products to find the product of 3 and 115?

_____ + _____ + _____ = _____

D. The stage manager buys _____ nails.

Connect to Vocabulary

A **partial product** is a product that results when the ones, tens, hundreds, and so on are multiplied separately. The partial products are then added together to find the whole product.

Step It Out

2 ▸ The production assistant prints 525 copies of the program for the play. Each program uses 4 sheets of paper. How many sheets of paper will be used?

Find 4 × 525. Use expanded form.

A. Write 525 in expanded form.

4 × 525 = 4 × (_____ + _____ + _____)

B. Use the Distributive Property.

4 × 525 = (_____ × _____) + (_____ × _____) + (_____ × _____)

C. Multiply to find each partial product. Use the grid to record the partial products, starting with the greatest place. Then add to find the whole product.

(_____ × _____) =
Think: partial product

(_____ × _____) =
Think: partial product

(_____ × _____) = +
Think: partial product

Think: product

D. _____ sheets of paper will be used.

· ·

Check Understanding   Math Board

324 inches

Use expanded form to find the product.

1 Amber has 4 rolls of ribbon. How many inches of ribbon does Amber have?

_____

_____

2 6 × 219 = _____   **3** 8 × 175 = _____

On Your Own

School Lunch Menu

MONDAY
Fun Fish Nuggets
TUESDAY
Oven-Grilled Hotdog
WEDNESDAY
Pazzo Bread with Dipping Sauce
THURSDAY
Cheese Pizza
FRIDAY
Fresh Hand-Breaded
Chicken Tenders

Use expanded form to find the product.

4 A school cafeteria serves 437 lunches in one day. If they serve the same number of lunches for 5 days, how many lunches will they serve?

_____

_____

5 (MP) **Reason** Tressa needs 1,800 small tiles to complete a mosaic. She buys 7 packages with 288 tiles in each package. Will she have enough tiles?

_____

_____

_____

6 **Open Ended** Use the digits 2, 4, 7, and 9 to write a 3-digit by 1-digit multiplication equation. Then find the product.

_____

_____

Use expanded form to find the product.

7 4 × 539

8 7 × 83

9 9 × 222

_____   _____   _____

🖩 I'm in a Learning Mindset!

How did I plan my solution to Task 1?

_____

_____

Name _____

Multiply Using Partial Products

(I Can) record partial products to multiply a multi-digit number by a 1-digit number.

Spark Your Learning

The Monstrosity Roller Coaster has seats for 136 riders. The roller coaster completes 4 runs each half hour. If all the seats on the roller coaster are filled each run, how many people can ride in a half hour?

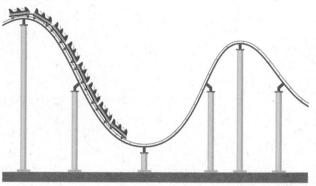

SMALL GROUPS

_____ can ride the roller coaster in a half hour.

Turn and Talk How can you use place value to help you multiply?

Build Understanding

1 On Saturday, 264 people ride a carousel in the park. On Sunday, 3 times as many people ride the carousel. How many people ride the carousel on Sunday?

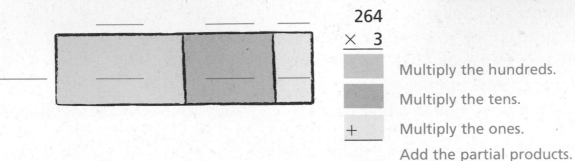

264
× 3

Multiply the hundreds.

Multiply the tens.

+   Multiply the ones.

Add the partial products.

A. What is the first step for showing the problem in an area model?

_____

B. Why do you multiply the hundreds first?

_____

_____

Write the partial products in each section of the area model.

C. How can you use place value to help you record the partial products and find the whole product?

_____

_____

D. How many people rode the carousel on Sunday? _____

E. How can you determine if your answer is reasonable?

_____

_____

Name _____

Step It Out

2 Treetop Academy is ordering notebooks for each of their 2,356 students. How many notebooks should they order?

> TREETOP ACADEMY
> 1. 4 notebooks for each student

Use what you know about expanded form, partial products, and place value to find the product.

A. Multiply: _____ × _____ Estimate: _____

B. Use expanded form to break apart the greater factor.

_____ + _____ + _____ + _____

C. Multiply and record the partial products. Then add the partial products.

$$2,356$$
$$\times \quad 4$$

4 × 2,000 ⟶ ☐

4 × _____ ⟶ ☐

_____ × _____ ⟶ ☐

_____ × _____ ⟶ + ☐

☐ notebooks

D. Is your answer reasonable? Explain.

_____

Check Understanding 🟦 Math Board

Estimate. Then use partial products to find the product.

1 Estimate: _____
34
× 7

2 Estimate: _____
496
× 3

3 Estimate: _____
2,581
× 9

On Your Own

4 **Social Studies** In 1908, President Theodore Roosevelt declared the Grand Canyon in Arizona a national monument. By 1919, the Grand Canyon became a national park. Zach, Kate, Dani, and Kito take a trip to visit the Grand Canyon. How much does the trip

cost the 4 friends? _____

TAKE A TRIP
TO SEE THE

GRAND CANYON

JUST
$397
per person

Estimate. Then use partial products to find the product.

5 Estimate: _____
   57
  × 8
   ‾‾‾

6 Estimate: _____
   291
  × 6
   ‾‾‾

7 Estimate: _____
   3,684
  ×   5
   ‾‾‾‾

Estimate. Then rewrite the problem vertically and use partial products to find the product.

8 Estimate: _____

3 × 195

9 Estimate: _____

9 × 76

10 Estimate: _____

7 × 2,408

I'm in a Learning Mindset!

How do I get back on track if I become distracted?

_____

Name _____

Use Place Value to Multiply 2-Digit Numbers

(I Can) use place value and regrouping to multiply a 2-digit number by a 1-digit number.

Spark Your Learning

Ramy is in a swim club that helps children learn about competitive swimming. In one race, he swims 4 laps of the pool. Each lap is 24 feet long. How far does Ramy swim during the race?

Show your thinking.

Ramy swims _____ feet.

Turn and Talk How can thinking about place value help you solve this problem?

Build Understanding

1 For the standing long jump, Gwen lands a jump that measures 24 inches. Amelia's jump is 2 times the length of Gwen's jump. What is the measure of Amelia's jump?

A. How can you use base-ten blocks to show 2 × 24? Draw a quick picture to show your answer.

B. Use what you know about place value to write 2 × 24 vertically.

Estimate. 2 × 24 is about _____.

Record the numbers.

C. When you multiply the ones, how can you record

2 × 4 ones? _____

D. When you multiply the tens, how can you record

2 × 2 tens? _____

E. Amelia's jump measures _____.

Turn and Talk How do you know if your answer is reasonable?

Step It Out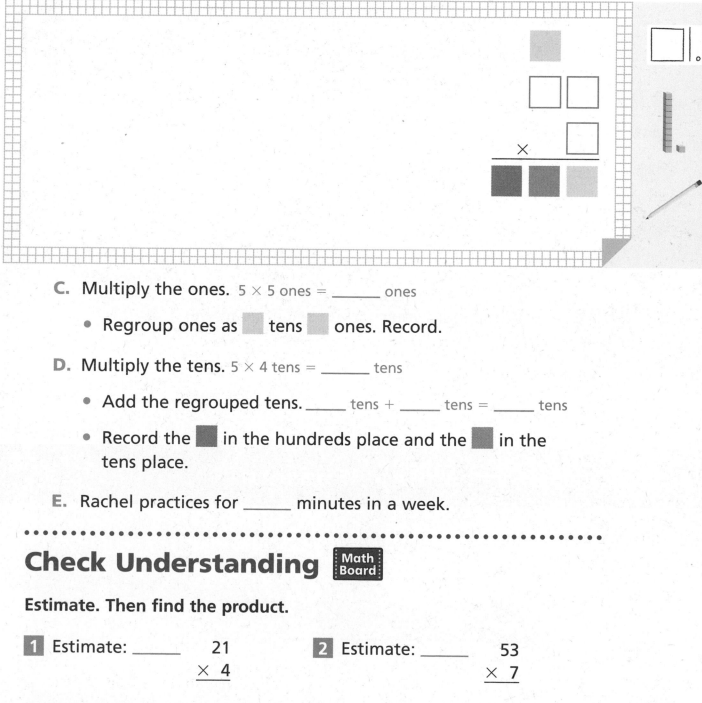

2 Rachel practices swimming 5 days a week. Each practice lasts for 45 minutes. How many minutes does Rachel practice in a week?

A. Use base-ten blocks to show 5 × 45.
Draw a quick picture to show your work.

B. Write the problem vertically, lining up the digits by place value.

C. Multiply the ones. 5 × 5 ones = _____ ones

- Regroup ones as ▉ tens ▉ ones. Record.

D. Multiply the tens. 5 × 4 tens = _____ tens

- Add the regrouped tens. _____ tens + _____ tens = _____ tens

- Record the ▉ in the hundreds place and the ▉ in the tens place.

E. Rachel practices for _____ minutes in a week.

Check Understanding 🟦 Math Board

Estimate. Then find the product.

1 Estimate: _____   21
                          × 4

2 Estimate: _____   53
                          × 7

On Your Own

3 The Gladiators scored twice as many points as the Patriots. How many points did the Gladiators score?

PATRIOTS GLADIATORS

_____

Estimate. Then find the product.

4 Estimate: _____

31
× 4

5 Estimate: _____

65
× 9

6 Estimate: _____

48
× 5

Estimate. Write the problem vertically and solve.

7 Estimate: _____

8 × 96

8 Estimate: _____

3 × 52

9 Estimate: _____

6 × 83

10 (MP) **Reason** Why should you check to see if an answer is reasonable?

_____

_____

🔢 I'm in a Learning Mindset!

What was the biggest challenge you faced in this lesson? How did you overcome it?

_____

_____

Name _____

Multiply 3-Digit and 4-Digit Numbers

(I Can) Use the standard algorithm to find the product of a multi-digit number and a single-digit number.

Spark Your Learning

Susan ran 1,423 feet on a track. David ran 3 times as far as Susan. How can you determine how far David ran?

Show your thinking.

David ran _____ feet.

Turn and Talk How can you use expanded form to multiply a 3-digit number by a 1-digit number?

Build Understanding

1 Dion has 3 full coin-collection books.
Each book holds the same number of
coins. How many coins does Dion have?

Draw a quick picture to show the problem.

A. How can you use what you know about place value
to write 3×104 vertically?

B. When you multiply the ones, how do you record
3×4 ones?

_____

C. What step is next?

_____

D. When you multiply the hundreds, how do you record
3×1 hundred?

_____

E. Dion has _____ coins.

 Turn and Talk How does using base-ten blocks show
that addition and multiplication are related?

© Houghton Mifflin Harcourt Publishing Company

Step It Out

2 ▶ Lisa challenges Carlos to read 7,137 words a day for 7 days. How many words is that?

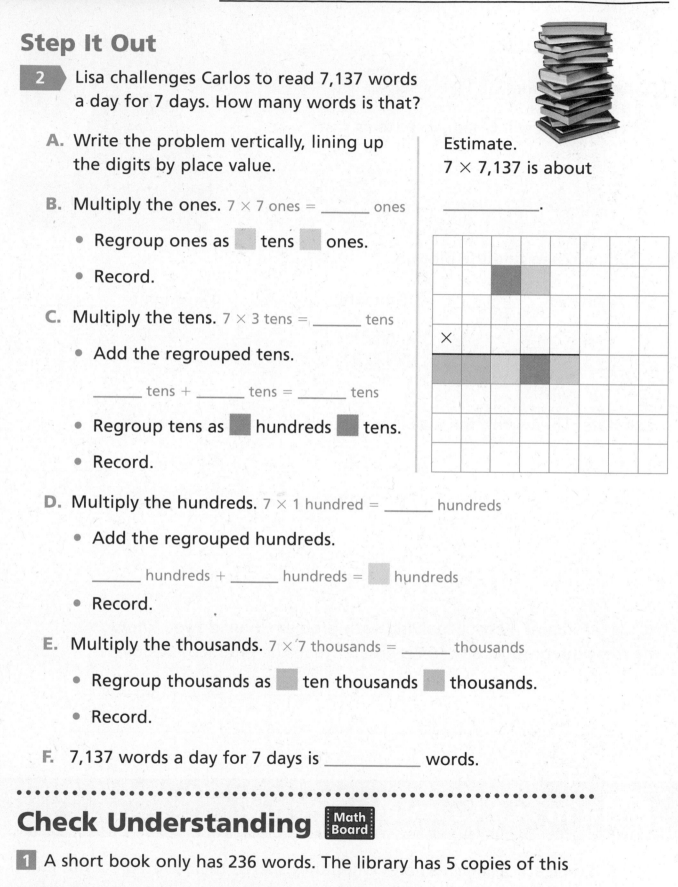

A. Write the problem vertically, lining up the digits by place value.

Estimate.
$7 \times 7{,}137$ is about

_____.

B. Multiply the ones. 7×7 ones = _____ ones

- Regroup ones as ☐ tens ☐ ones.

- Record.

C. Multiply the tens. 7×3 tens = _____ tens

- Add the regrouped tens.

  _____ tens + _____ tens = _____ tens

- Regroup tens as ☐ hundreds ☐ tens.

- Record.

D. Multiply the hundreds. 7×1 hundred = _____ hundreds

- Add the regrouped hundreds.

  _____ hundreds + _____ hundreds = ☐ hundreds

- Record.

E. Multiply the thousands. 7×7 thousands = _____ thousands

- Regroup thousands as ☐ ten thousands ☐ thousands.

- Record.

F. 7,137 words a day for 7 days is _____ words.

Check Understanding 〔Math Board〕

1 A short book only has 236 words. The library has 5 copies of this book. How many words appear in the books? _____

On Your Own

Show your work.

2 How much will 6 gaming systems cost? _____

$327

Estimate. Then find the product.

3 Estimate: _____

$$\begin{array}{r} 754 \\ \times\ \ \ 3 \\ \hline \end{array}$$

4 Estimate: _____

$$\begin{array}{r} 6{,}821 \\ \times\ \ \ \ \ 5 \\ \hline \end{array}$$

5 Estimate: _____

$$\begin{array}{r} 4{,}932 \\ \times\ \ \ \ \ 9 \\ \hline \end{array}$$

Estimate. Then write the problem vertically and find the product.

6 Estimate: _____

6×523

7 Estimate: _____

$9 \times 5{,}181$

8 Estimate: _____

$8 \times 6{,}719$

9 (MP) **Reason** Without solving each problem, how do you know that the product 8×564 is greater than the product 7×564?

_____

_____

✳ I'm in a Learning Mindset!

What did I learn from classmates when they shared their strategies with me?

_____

Name _____

Use Equations to Solve Multistep Problems

(I Can) Use equations to solve multistep problems.

Spark Your Learning

The apple trees grew so many apples that Lia filled 7 baskets with 13 apples each to take to the school picnic. Once there, Lia gave apples to everyone who passed by. At the end of the day, she had 46 apples left. How many apples did she pass out?

PAIRS

Lia passed out _____ apples.

Turn and Talk How were your steps for solving the problem alike or different?

Build Understanding

1 Malik collects stamps in an album that has 48 pages.
He puts 8 stamps on each of the first 6 pages.
He puts 15 stamps on each of the next 9 pages.
How many stamps are in Malik's album?

A. How can you show what is happening in the problem?

_____

_____

B. Is there any extra information in the problem that you do not need?

_____

C. What will the answer tell us?

_____

D. What do you need to do first to solve the problem?

_____

_____

E. About how many stamps do you think there are? Why?

_____

_____

F. Show how you can solve the problem.

There are _____ stamps in Malik's album.

Turn and Talk How does your answer compare with your estimate?

© Houghton Mifflin Harcourt Publishing Company

Step It Out

2 On Monday and Tuesday, Anne bikes to the beach and back home. On Thursday and Friday, Anne bikes to the park and back home. How many miles does Anne ride her bike?

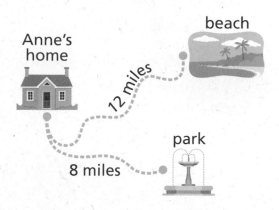

Anne's home

beach

12 miles

park

8 miles

A. Underline the information you need to solve the problem.

B. Write an equation to model the number of miles Anne bikes to and from each location.

beach: _____

park: _____

Let *m* = the miles Anne bikes *Monday* and *Tuesday*.
Let *n* = the miles Anne bikes *Thursday* and *Friday*.

C. How can you write an equation to find the number of miles Anne bikes? Use the order of operations to solve the problem. Let *t* = the total number of miles Anne bikes.

> **Connect to Vocabulary**
>
> The **order of operations** is a set of rules that gives the order in which calculations are done. From left to right, first multiply and divide, and then add and subtract.

D. Anne rides her bike _____.

• •

Check Understanding

Find the product. Show your work.

1 Corey goes to a store with $25 to spend. He buys 3 packages of baseball cards. Each package costs $6. How much money

does Corey have now? _____

Let *c* = the money Corey has left.

On Your Own

2 (MP) **Model with Mathematics** Evan has 4 pieces of rope that are the same length. He needs 75 feet of rope to build a bridge. How much more rope does Evan need?

13 feet

- What do you need to do first to solve the problem?

  _____

- Write an equation to find the answer to the first step. Then solve. Let f = the total length of rope Evan already has.

  _____

- About how much more rope does Evan need?

  _____

- Write an equation to find exactly how much more rope Evan needs. Then solve. Let n = the length of rope Evan needs.

  _____

  Evan needs _____ more feet of rope.

- Explain why your answer is reasonable.

  _____

Use the order of operations and find the value of n.

3 $40 \times 8 - 7 \times 3 = n$ **4** $32 + 2 \times 35 - 8 = n$

_____ $= n$ _____ $= n$

×÷ I'm in a Learning Mindset!

What do I do when I do not know what to do?

_____

Review

Vocabulary

Choose the correct term from the Vocabulary box to complete the sentence.

1 _____ is a method of multiplying in which the ones, tens, hundreds, and so on are multiplied separately and then the products are added together.

2 _____ is a special set of rules which gives the order in which calculations are done.

Concepts and Skills

3 (MP) **Use Tools** An oak tree in the park is 85 feet tall. Julie reads about some trees that can grow to be 3 times as tall as the oak tree. How tall would those trees be? Tell what strategy or tool you will use to answer the question, explain your choice, and then find the answer.

_____

_____

4 Draw an area model to represent the product. Record the product. 4 × 12 = _____

5 Draw a quick picture to find the product.

4 × 13 = _____

Draw a quick picture to show the product.

6 3×24 **7** 2×111 **8** 2×43

9 Our plan is to drive 123 miles a day for 5 days to get to Orlando. How many miles will we drive? Use expanded form to find the product.

_____

10 Which correctly shows the partial products that can be used to find the answer? Select all that apply.

(A)
```
   21
×   4
─────
   80
+   4
─────
   84
```

(B)
```
  165
×   8
─────
  800
   48
+  40
─────
  888
```

(C)
```
 3,472
×     6
───────
18,000
 2,400
   420
+    12
───────
20,832
```

(D)
```
   63
×   9
─────
   27
+  54
─────
   81
```

(E)
```
  186
×   7
─────
  700
   56
+  42
─────
  798
```

11 Which correctly shows the product? Select all that apply.

(A)
```
  467
×   7
─────
3,269
```

(B)
```
 2,105
×     8
──────
16,840
```

(C)
```
  408
×   5
─────
2,004
```

(D)
```
 5,673
×     6
──────
33,638
```

(E)
```
 3,782
×     3
──────
11,346
```

12 There are 11 markers in each of 2 jars on the table. There are 26 markers in the box on the shelf. How many markers are there?

(A) 48   (B) 63   (C) 288   (D) 338

Understand Division by 1-Digit Numbers

How many are missing?

- Students in science class work in pairs. There are 10 pairs of students. The teacher wants each pair to get 4 pine cones.

- Circle as many groups of 4 pine cones as you can. How many groups did you make? _____

- How many more pine cones are needed so that every pair of students has 4? _____

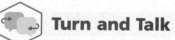 **Turn and Talk**

- How might you arrange the pine cones to make it easier to find the number of groups of 4?

- How would your answer change if the science teacher wanted each pair to get 5 pine cones?

Are You Ready?

Complete these problems to review prior concepts and skills
you will need for this module.

Relate Division to Subtraction

Complete the jumps on the number line to find 9 ÷ 3.

1 You subtract 3 _____ times. 9 ÷ 3 = _____

Meaning of Division: Equal Groups

Divide to find the number in each group.

2 Manuel has 24 flowers. He wants to fill 4 vases,
each with the same number of flowers. How many
flowers will be in each vase?

Circle equal groups of flowers.

There are _____ groups of flowers.

There are _____ flowers in each group.

Manuel will put _____ flowers in each vase.

Meaning of Division: Arrays

Make an array to help solve the problem.

3 You have 18 tiles. You make
3 equal rows. How many tiles
are in each row?

4 You have 20 tiles. You want to put
5 in each row. How many rows
will you have?

There are _____ tiles in each row.

I will have _____ rows of tiles.

Name _____

Represent Division

(I Can) use visual models and equations to represent division problems.

Spark Your Learning

Gene and Stephanie are playing a word game with these letter tiles. To start, they place all the tiles in 2 equal rows.

Show how many tiles are in each row.

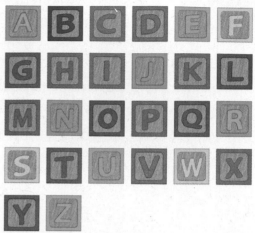

Turn and Talk How does your representation show division?

Build Understanding

1 Teresa fills 42 water balloons for a water balloon race. Each player needs 3 balloons. How many players are in the race?

Use counters or tiles to represent the problem. Then draw a visual model to show your work.

A. How did you represent the number of balloons Teresa fills? _____

B. How did you represent the number of balloons each player needs? _____

C. How can you use your representation to find the number of players? _____

_____

D. How many players are in the race? _____

 Turn and Talk How can you write a division equation to model the problem?

2 A memory game requires 55 cards. Beth places the cards in 5 equal rows. How many cards are in each row?

Use base-ten blocks to represent the problem. Then use the quick picture to solve the problem.

A. How does the quick picture represent the problem?

_____

_____

B. How does the quick picture show the answer?

_____

_____

C. What division equation can you write to model the problem? _____

D. How many cards are in each row? _____

 Turn and Talk Why can you also write a multiplication equation to model this problem?

• •

Check Understanding 〔Math Board〕

Draw a visual model and write a division equation to represent the problem. Then solve.

1 There are 48 players in a sack race. The players are in 4 equal teams. How many players are on each team?

2 A basketball player makes 93 points from 3-point shots. How many 3-point shots does the player make?

On Your Own

3 (MP) **Use Structure** Paula has this pitcher of juice. She also has glasses that each hold 8 fluid ounces. How many glasses can she fill? Draw a visual model and write an equation to represent the division. Then solve.

88 fluid ounces

_____

4 (MP) **Model with Mathematics** Vanessa finds 3 clues in a treasure hunt and gets 39 points. Each clue is worth the same number of points. Vanessa draws this quick picture to represent how many points each clue is worth. Write a division equation to model the problem. Then solve.

_____

5 **Open Ended** Write and solve a division word problem that can be represented by the array.

_____

_____

_____

⬡ I'm in a Learning Mindset!

What questions can I ask my teacher to help me understand how to represent division?

_____

_____

© Houghton Mifflin Harcourt Publishing Company • Image Credit: ©Shutterstock

Name _____

Investigate Remainders

(I Can) use visual models to identify the whole-number quotient and remainder in a division problem.

Spark Your Learning

Edwin is setting up tables and chairs for a party. There are 22 chairs. He must put the same number of chairs at each of these tables. How many chairs can Edwin put at each table?

Show your thinking.

SMALL GROUPS

Turn and Talk Are there any chairs that Edwin does *not* put at the tables? Why or why not?

Build Understanding

1 Patrick needs 4 pinwheels to make each decoration for the party. He has 25 pinwheels. How many decorations can Patrick make? How many pinwheels will be left over?

Use counters or tiles to represent the problem. Then draw a visual model to show your work.

A. How did you represent all of the pinwheels?

_____

B. How did you represent the number of pinwheels in

each decoration? _____

C. How can you use your representation to find the number of decorations that Patrick can make?

_____

D. How can you use your representation to find the number of pinwheels that are left over?

_____

E. Patrick can make _____ decorations and _____ pinwheel will be left over.

 Turn and Talk How can you use the relationship between division and multiplication to check that your answer is reasonable?

2 Elise has 35 pencils to make 8 party bags. She puts the same number of pencils in each bag. How many pencils does Elise put in each bag? How many pencils are left over?

A. Draw an array to represent 35 ÷ 8.

B. How does the array show how many pencils are in each party bag?

_____

_____

C. How does the array show how many pencils are left over?

_____

_____

D. The whole-number quotient is _____ and the remainder is _____, or 4 r3.

 Turn and Talk Why is there a remainder in this problem?

> **Connect to Vocabulary**
>
> When a number cannot be divided evenly, the amount that is left over is called the **remainder**. To record the answer, write the whole-number quotient, then the letter r, and then the remainder.

• •

Check Understanding `Math Board`

1 Leslie blows up 24 balloons. She will tie 9 balloons together to make a bouquet. How many bouquets can Leslie make? How many balloons will be left over? Draw a visual model to solve the problem.

_____

On Your Own

2 (MP) **Use Tools** Ms. Ritchie has 42 sheets of paper for an art project. Each student needs 5 sheets. How many students can get paper? How many sheets are left over?

Use counters or tiles to represent and solve the problem.

_____ students get paper. _____ sheets are left over.

Write the whole-number quotient and remainder.

3 27 ÷ 4

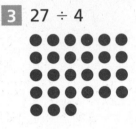

whole-number quotient _____

remainder _____

4 36 ÷ 7

• • • • • • •
• • • • • • •
• • • • • • •
• • • • • • •
• • • • • • • •

whole-number quotient _____

remainder _____

5 (MP) **Reason** Draw a visual model for 17 ÷ 3. What is the remainder? How do you know?

_____

_____

😀➗ I'm in a Learning Mindset!

How did using a visual model help me understand how to divide numbers that do not divide evenly?

_____

_____

Name _____

Interpret Remainders

(I Can) solve a division problem and interpret the remainder in the context of the problem.

Spark Your Learning

Aiden is building solar toy cars in his science club. The cars collect and use energy from the sun for power. Aiden buys 18 wheels. Each car needs 4 wheels. How many cars can Aiden build?

Show your thinking.

PAIRS

Turn and Talk What is the remainder in this problem? What does the remainder mean?

Build Understanding

1 There are 57 students going to the science museum. Each van can take 5 students. How many vans are needed to take all the students?

Use a visual model to show how the students are divided into groups of 5.

A. For 57 ÷ 5, the whole-number quotient is _____ and the

remainder is _____, or _____ r_____.

B. What does the whole-number quotient mean in this problem?

_____

C. What does the remainder mean in this problem?

_____

D. How can you use the whole-number quotient and the remainder to solve the problem?

_____

_____

E. To take all the students, _____ vans are needed.

 Turn and Talk How can you use the whole-number quotient and remainder to answer these questions? *How many vans will be full? How many students will ride in the van that is not full?*

142

Step It Out

2 Amanda has 73 inches of wire for a science experiment. She needs to cut all the wire into 8 identical pieces. How many inches long will each piece be?

A. Draw an array to show 73 divided into 8 equal groups.

B. For 73 ÷ 8, the whole-number quotient is

_____ and the remainder is _____.

C. The remainder represents the amount of wire left over. Divide that amount into 8 equal groups and write the result as a fraction of a whole inch.

[whole-number quotient] $\dfrac{[remainder]}{[divisor]}$ = ☐ $\dfrac{☐}{☐}$

D. Each piece of wire will be _____ inches long.

 Turn and Talk Why is this problem a good situation to write the remainder as a fraction?

Check Understanding [Math Board]

1 Maya needs 44 batteries for smoke alarms. The batteries come in packs of 6. How many packs does Maya need to buy?

- For 44 ÷ 6, the whole-number quotient

  is _____ and the remainder is _____.

- Maya needs to buy _____ packs.

- Circle how you interpreted the remainder to solve the problem.

Four Ways to Interpret a Remainder

1. Use only the whole-number quotient.
2. Use only the remainder.
3. Add 1 to the whole-number quotient to account for the remainder.
4. Include the remainder as a fraction.

On Your Own

(MP) **Use Tools** Use objects or draw visual models to represent each division problem. Then explain how you interpreted the remainder to solve the problem.

2 Tara wants to have 30 slices of pizza for a party so that each person can have 2 slices. How many of these pizzas does Tara need to order?

_____

_____

_____

3 Izra rides his bike 45 miles in 4 days. He rides the same distance each day. How many miles does Izra ride each day?

_____

_____

_____

4 Desiree makes 56 candles to sell at the county fair. She packs as many of these boxes as possible. How many boxes can Desiree fill?

_____

_____

_____

⬡ I'm in a Learning Mindset!

What parts of interpreting remainders can I do on my own? What parts do I need help with?

_____

Name _____

Use Area Models and the Distributive Property to Divide

(I Can) solve multi-digit division problems using area models and the Distributive Property.

Spark Your Learning

Shawn is building a rectangular pen for holding sheep. The area of the pen needs to be 63 square feet, and the pen must be 3 feet wide. How long should the pen be?

Show your thinking.

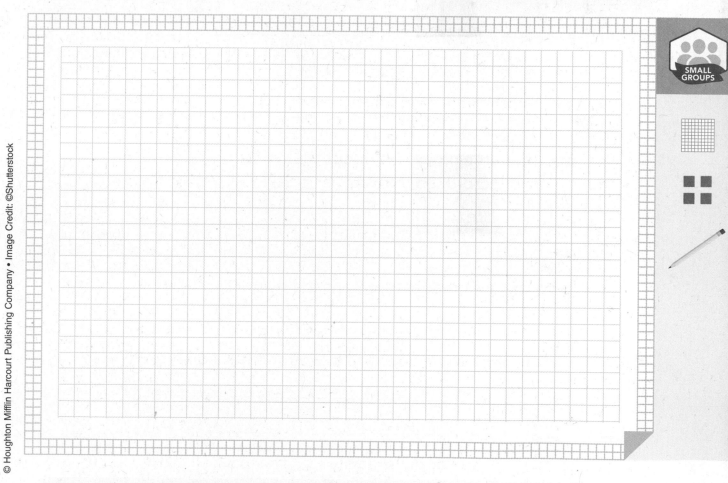

SMALL GROUPS

Turn and Talk How can thinking about multiplication help you solve this area problem?

Build Understanding

1 Reggie shears sheep for their wool. He places all the wool in this bag. Each sheep provides 4 kilograms of wool. How many sheep does Reggie shear?

92 KILOGRAMS

Find 92 ÷ 4.

A. How can you break apart 92 into smaller parts that are easier to divide by 4?

92 = 80 + _____

92 ÷ 4 = (_____ + _____) ÷ 4

B. Complete the area model representing the division.

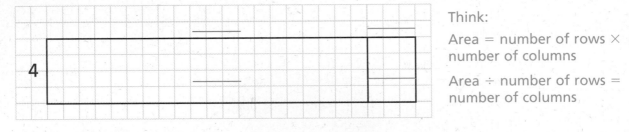

4

Think:

Area = number of rows × number of columns

Area ÷ number of rows = number of columns

C. How does the area model represent the whole dividend and the dividend broken into smaller parts?

_____

_____

D. How does the area model represent the divisor?

_____

E. How does it show the whole-number quotient is equal to 20 + 3?

_____

_____

F. 92 ÷ 4 = _____, so Reggie shears _____ sheep.

Turn and Talk How can you use multiplication and the area model to check your answer?

Step It Out

2 Use an area model and the Distributive Property to find 217 ÷ 7.

A. Break apart 217 into numbers that are easier to divide by 7.

217 = _____ + _____

B. Use the easier numbers to divide.

217 ÷ 7 = (_____ + _____) ÷ 7

= (_____ ÷ 7) + (_____ ÷ 7)

= _____ + _____

= _____

> ### Connect to Vocabulary
>
> The **Distributive Property** states that multiplying a sum by a number is the same as multiplying each addend by the number and then adding the products. Example:
> (10 + 8) × 2 = (10 × 2) + (8 × 2)
> The Distributive Property also applies to division. Example:
> (10 + 8) ÷ 2 = (10 ÷ 2) + (8 ÷ 2)

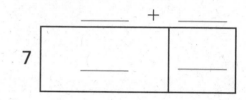

·······································

Check Understanding [Math Board]

1 Ajay has 54 pounds of wool. He uses 3 pounds to make a blanket. How many blankets can he make? Use an area model to find 54 ÷ 3.

Ajay can make _____ blankets.

Use the Distributive Property to divide.

2 72 ÷ 4

= (_____ + _____) ÷ 4

= (_____ ÷ 4) + (_____ ÷ 4)

= _____ + _____

= _____

3 115 ÷ 5

= (_____ + _____) ÷ 5

= (_____ ÷ 5) + (_____ ÷ 5)

= _____ + _____

= _____

On Your Own

4 (MP) **Use Tools** Debra raises alpacas for their wool. She feeds each alpaca 7 pounds of food each week. She uses 98 pounds of food each week. How many alpacas does Debra have? Use an area model to find 98 ÷ 7.

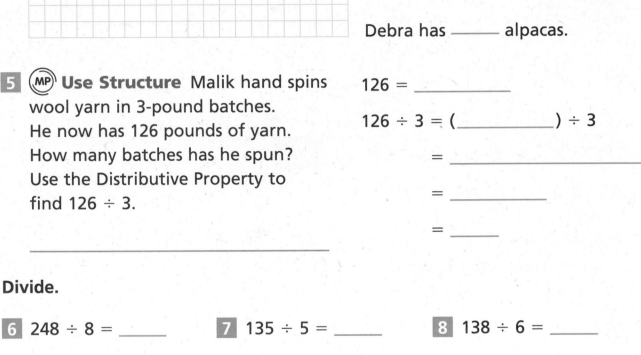

Debra has _____ alpacas.

5 (MP) **Use Structure** Malik hand spins wool yarn in 3-pound batches. He now has 126 pounds of yarn. How many batches has he spun? Use the Distributive Property to find 126 ÷ 3.

_____

126 = _____

126 ÷ 3 = (_____) ÷ 3

= _____

= _____

= _____

Divide.

6 248 ÷ 8 = _____

7 135 ÷ 5 = _____

8 138 ÷ 6 = _____

⬡ **I'm in a Learning Mindset!**

How did using an area model help me understand using the Distributive Property to divide?

_____

Name _____

Divide Using Repeated Subtraction

(I Can) write an equation to represent a division problem and use repeated subtraction to solve.

Spark Your Learning

Lisa buys 32 energy bars for swim meets. She brings 4 bars to each meet. How many meets can Lisa go to before all the bars are gone?

Use a visual model to represent and solve the problem.

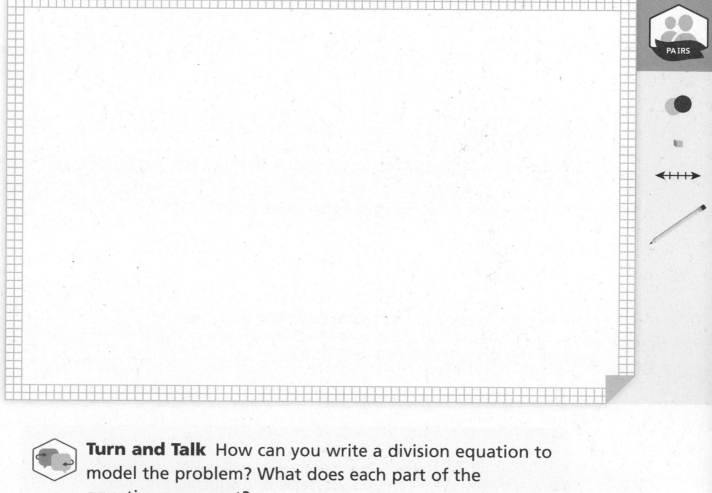

PAIRS

Turn and Talk How can you write a division equation to model the problem? What does each part of the equation represent?

Build Understanding

1 Lisa's swimming coach has $50 to spend on this pair of goggles. How many pairs of goggles can the coach buy?

Swimdeals
Shopping basket

Price Quantity

$8 1 ⬍

Subtotal:
$8.00

Swim goggles

⊖ CHECKOUT

A. For each pair of goggles that the coach buys, what happens to the amount of money that he has to spend?

_____

B. Why can you use subtraction to show that process?

_____

C. Show how you can solve using repeated subtraction.

D. How many pairs of goggles can the coach buy? _____

How do you know? _____

_____

E. How much money will the coach have left after he

buys all the goggles he can with $50? _____

F. For 50 ÷ 8, the whole number quotient is _____ and

the remainder is _____, or _____ r _____.

 Turn and Talk Why can you use repeated subtraction to divide?

Step It Out

2 Coach Rivera has 36 nose clips to give to members of her synchronized swimming team. Each swimmer gets 5 clips. How many swimmers are on the team?

A. Write a division equation to model the problem.

_____

B. Use repeated subtraction to divide. Start with the dividend. Subtract the divisor as many times as you can.

C. Count the number of times you subtract the divisor to find the whole-number quotient. Any amount left over is the remainder.

D. There are _____ swimmers on the team.

```
3 6    ← dividend
- 5    1 time
3 1
- 5    2 times
2 6
- 5    _____ times
2 1
- 5    _____ times
1 6
- 5    _____ times
1 1
- 5    _____ times
6
- 5    _____ times
1    ← remainder
```

 Turn and Talk Could you subtract multiples of the divisor to divide? Why or why not?

Check Understanding 〔Math Board〕

1 There are 46 swimmers and 7 lanes. The same number of swimmers will go in each lane. Any remaining swimmers will practice diving. How many swimmers will each lane have?

• Write a division equation to model the problem.

_____

• Use the space at the right to show how you can use repeated subtraction to solve.

Each lane will have _____ swimmers.

On Your Own

2 (MP) **Model with Mathematics** There are 84 campers going on a whitewater rafting trip. Each raft can fit 6 campers. How many rafts are needed for all the campers? Write a division equation to model the problem. Use repeated subtraction to divide.

_____

Use repeated subtraction to divide.

3 96 ÷ 8 _____

4 46 ÷ 5 _____

5 (MP) **Use Tools** Use the number line to show how to use repeated subtraction to find 40 ÷ 7.

For 40 ÷ 7, the whole-number quotient is _____ and the

remainder is _____, or _____ r_____.

I'm in a Learning Mindset!

What is still unclear to me about using repeated subtraction to divide?

_____

Name _____

Divide Using Partial Quotients

(**I Can**) use partial quotients to divide multi-digit numbers by
1-digit numbers.

Spark Your Learning

At an airport, shuttle buses take
passengers from the parking lot to the
terminal. To transport 96 passengers,
4 shuttle buses are needed. How many
passengers can fit on each bus?

Show your thinking.

SMALL
GROUPS

 Turn and Talk What are two different ways that you
can break apart 96 to make it easier to divide by 4?

Build Understanding

1 An airplane has 165 seats. There are 5 seats in each row. How many rows of seats are there?

Draw an area model to represent 165 ÷ 5.

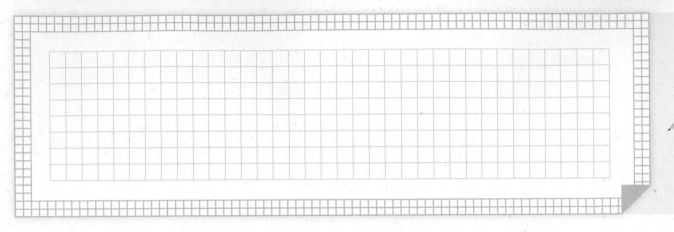

A. How did you break apart 165 into smaller parts that are multiples of 5?

165 = _____

B. How can you divide each smaller part of the dividend to find a smaller part of the whole-number quotient?

_____

_____

C. Each smaller part of the whole-number quotient is called a partial quotient. How can you use these partial quotients to find 165 ÷ 5?

_____

_____

D. There are _____ rows of seats.

 Turn and Talk How does using partial quotients to divide relate to using an area model to represent the division?

> ### Connect to Vocabulary
>
> In the **partial quotient** method of dividing, multiples of the divisor are subtracted from the dividend and then the partial quotients are added together.

Step It Out

2 Use partial quotients to find 862 ÷ 7.

partial quotients

A. Find a multiple of the divisor that is less than or equal to the dividend.

7 × 100 = _____

B. Subtract that multiple from the dividend.

C. Keep subtracting multiples of the divisor until the remaining number is less than the divisor. That remaining number is the remainder.

D. Add all the partial quotients to find the whole-number quotient.

100 + 20 + 3 = _____

862 ÷ 7 is _____ r _____.

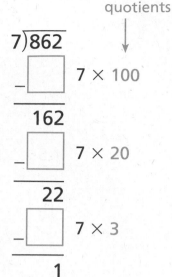

$7\overline{)862}$
- ☐   7 × 100
162
- ☐   7 × 20
22
- ☐   7 × 3
1

Turn and Talk How does using partial quotients to divide relate to using repeated subtraction to divide?

- -

Check Understanding [Math Board]

MINI PRETZELS   SALTED PEANUTS

1 Hank loads 848 snack packs onto 4 airplanes. He puts the same number of packs on each plane. How many packs does Hank put on each airplane? Use partial quotients to find 848 ÷ 4.

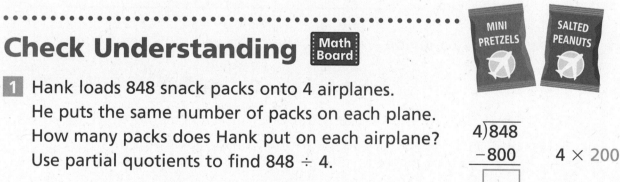

200

| 4 | 800 | 40 | 8 |

_____ ____

$4\overline{)848}$
−800   4 × 200
☐
−☐   4 × _____
☐
☐
−☐   4 × _____
☐

200 + _____ + _____ = _____

Hank loads _____ snack packs on each plane.

© Houghton Mifflin Harcourt Publishing Company

On Your Own

2 (MP) **Attend to Precision** This airport parking garage has 5 floors. Each floor holds the same number of cars. How many cars can each floor hold? Use partial quotients to divide. Show your work.

$5\overline{)1{,}545}$

☐ ☐ ☐ 5×200

Each floor of the garage can hold _____ cars.

3 (MP) **Use Structure** Which problem is easier to solve using partial quotients? Why?

$693 \div 3 = \blacksquare$

$543 \div 3 = \blacksquare$

_____

_____

Use partial quotients to divide.

4 $248 \div 8$ _____

5 $185 \div 5$ _____

6 $740 \div 6$ _____

✕➗ I'm in a Learning Mindset!

What is still unclear to me about using partial quotients to divide?

_____

Module 6 Review

Vocabulary

Choose the correct term from the Vocabulary box to complete the sentence.

1 The amount left over after making equal groups is

called the _____.

2 The _____ states that multiplying (or dividing) a sum by a number is the same as multiplying (or dividing) each addend by the number and then adding the products (or quotients).

3 In the _____ method of dividing, multiples of the divisor are subtracted from the dividend.

Concepts and Skills

4 What division problem does this visual model represent? How do you know?

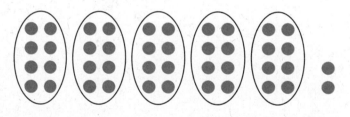

_____

_____

5 (MP) **Use Tools** Select all the division problems that have a remainder. Tell what strategy or tool you will use to solve the problem, explain your choice, and then find the answers.

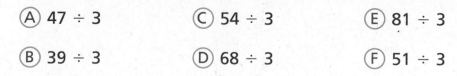

(A) $47 ÷ 3$ (C) $54 ÷ 3$ (E) $81 ÷ 3$

(B) $39 ÷ 3$ (D) $68 ÷ 3$ (F) $51 ÷ 3$

_____

_____

6 Gina makes 40 cups of vegetable broth. She pours the broth into 6 bowls, with the same amount in each bowl. How many cups of broth are in each bowl?

Ⓐ 5 cups   Ⓑ $5\frac{2}{3}$ cups   Ⓒ 6 cups   Ⓓ $6\frac{2}{3}$ cups

7 A golf coach buys 42 golf balls. He gives the same number of golf balls to each of his 4 students. He puts the leftover balls in his office. How many golf balls does the coach give to each student?

---

8 A chef makes 130 salads for an awards dinner. She can fit 4 salads on each tray. She fills as many trays as she can. Select all the correct statements about the salads.

Ⓐ 32 trays are full.   Ⓓ 1 tray has only 2 salads.

Ⓑ 1 tray has only 1 salad.   Ⓔ 33 trays are full.

Ⓒ She uses 33 trays.   Ⓕ She uses 32 trays.

Divide.

9 144 ÷ 8 _____

10 25 ÷ 3 _____

11 288 ÷ 7 _____

12 335 ÷ 5 _____

WHAT IS THE SECRET PHRASE?

- In each equation, the letter represents an unknown number.

- Find the value of the unknown number. Then write the letter above the value in the blanks below. When complete, you will reveal a secret phrase.

$64 \div 8 = V$	$I \div 5 = 7$	$O \div 3 = 9$
$18 \div D = 3$	$S \div 4 = 8$	$35 \div N = 7$
$36 \div 9 = I$	$56 \div G = 8$	$L \div 1 = 10$
$O \div 8 = 9$	$N \div 8 = 3$	$6 \div 3 = I$

___ ___ ___ ___
10 27 24 7

___ ___ ___ ___ ___ ___ ___
6   2   8   4   32 35 72 5

🐑 **Turn and Talk**

- What strategies did you use to find the unknown numbers?

Are You Ready?

Complete these problems to review prior concepts and skills you will need for this module.

Use Arrays to Divide

Make an array to show 24 ÷ 6. Then complete the statements.

1 Think: How many groups of _____ are in _____?

Draw the array.

I drew rows with _____ tiles in each row.

I drew _____ rows.

$24 \div 6 = $ _____

Multiply Whole Numbers

Find the product.

2 $\begin{array}{r} 15 \\ \times\ 4 \\ \hline \end{array}$

3 $\begin{array}{r} 43 \\ \times\ 7 \\ \hline \end{array}$

4 $\begin{array}{r} 28 \\ \times\ 6 \\ \hline \end{array}$

5 $\begin{array}{r} 27 \\ \times\ 5 \\ \hline \end{array}$

6 $\begin{array}{r} 32 \\ \times\ 3 \\ \hline \end{array}$

7 $\begin{array}{r} 55 \\ \times\ 8 \\ \hline \end{array}$

Subtract Through 4-Digit Numbers

Find the difference.

8 $\begin{array}{r} 293 \\ -\ 78 \\ \hline \end{array}$

9 $\begin{array}{r} 6,352 \\ -\ 891 \\ \hline \end{array}$

10 $\begin{array}{r} 1,437 \\ -\ 629 \\ \hline \end{array}$

Name _____

Represent Division with Regrouping

(I Can) represent and record division problems with a 1-digit divisor and regrouping.

Spark Your Learning

Dani manages a charter boat business. She has these fishing lures for 3 boats. She wants to put the same number of lures on each boat. How many lures should Dani put on each boat?

Show your thinking.

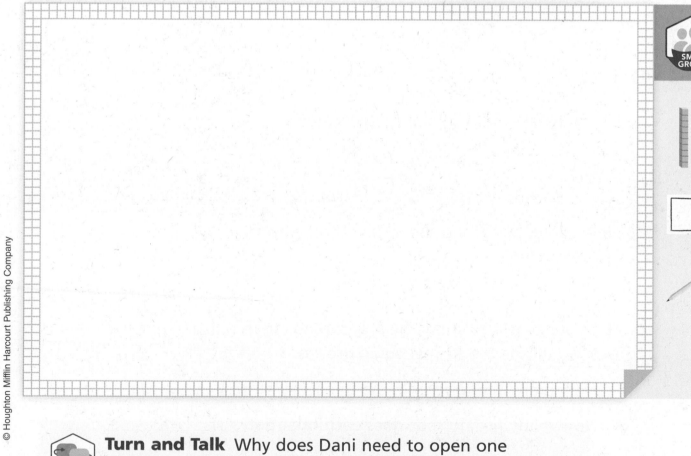

SMALL GROUPS

Turn and Talk Why does Dani need to open one package of lures in order to divide all the lures equally?

© Houghton Mifflin Harcourt Publishing Company

Build Understanding

1 Frank owns a charter boat business. He buys 56 fishing rods. Frank divides the rods equally among his 4 boats. How many fishing rods does each boat get?

Find 56 ÷ 4.

Use base-ten blocks to show 56 as 5 tens 6 ones. Try to put all the blocks into 4 equal groups. Draw a quick picture to show your work.

A. Which blocks are not in a group? Why?

_____

_____

B. How can you regroup the leftover ten with the leftover ones?

_____

C. Use your blocks to show the regrouping. Then finish putting all the blocks in 4 equal groups.

- How many tens and ones are in each group? _____

- How many fishing rods does each boat get? _____

 Turn and Talk How can regrouping 1 ten as 10 ones help when you divide?

Step It Out

2 Use quick pictures to represent division.

Find 85 ÷ 3.

The picture shows 85 as 8 tens 5 ones.
The 3 circles represent the equal groups.
Cross off tens and ones as you put them
into the groups.

A. Share the 8 tens equally among the 3 groups.

How many tens are in each group? _____

How many tens are left over? _____

```
      [ ]  ← tens in each group
  3)8 5
  -[ ]     ← tens used
   [ ]     ← tens left over
```

B. Regroup the leftover tens as ones.

How many ones are there now? _____

```
      2
  3)8 5
  -6 ↓
   [ ]   ← ones to share
```

C. Share the ones equally among the 3 groups.

How many ones are in each group? _____

How many ones are left over? _____

```
      2[ ]  ← ones in each group
  3)8 5
  -6
   2 5
  -[ ]   ← ones used
   [ ]   ← ones left over
```

D. Write the whole-number quotient and remainder.

85 ÷ 3 is _____ r _____.

Turn and Talk Why do you need to regroup in Step B?

Check Understanding [Math Board]

1 Lana has 76 sand dollars. She puts the same number in 4 boxes. How many sand dollars are in each box? Use base-ten blocks to represent the division. Record the results.

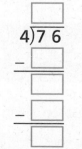

_____ sand dollars are in each box.

On Your Own

2 (MP) **Use Tools** Marco puts all of his scallop shells in 6 jars. He puts the same number in each jar. How many scallop shells are in each jar? Use base-ten blocks to represent the division. Then draw a quick picture to show your work.

Marco's Shell Collection	
Shell	**Number**
Augur	32
Scallop	96
Coquina	54

_____

(MP) **Use Tools** Use base-ten blocks or quick pictures to represent the division. Record the results.

3 56 ÷ 4 _____   **4** 85 ÷ 7 _____   **5** 38 ÷ 6 _____

6 **Open Ended** Write a division problem with a 2-digit dividend and a 1-digit divisor. The answer should be 15 r2. Draw a quick picture to show how to solve it.

_____

I'm in a Learning Mindset!

What tools can I use to help me regroup when dividing?

_____

Name _____

Use Place Value to Divide

(I Can) determine how many digits a whole-number quotient will have and use long division to divide.

Spark Your Learning

Aseem and Chadda have 316 photos to put in 2 scrapbooks. They agree to put the same number of photos in each book. But they disagree about how many photos that is.

Aseem: We can put more than 100 photos in each book.

Chadda: We don't have enough photos to put 100 in each book.

Who is right? Show and explain your thinking.

 Turn and Talk How many digits are in the whole-number quotient for 316 ÷ 2? Use place value to explain.

Build Understanding

1 Fran has 423 scrapbook stickers. She wants to put an equal number of stickers in 3 different scrapbooks. How many stickers can she put in each scrapbook?

Find 423 ÷ 3.

Use base-ten blocks to show the division.

A. Were there enough hundreds to put at least 1 hundred in each group? Why or why not?

_____

_____

B. How many digits are in the whole-number quotient when there is at least 1 hundred in each group? _____ digits

C. How many hundreds did you regroup as tens? _____ hundred

How many tens did you put in each group? _____ tens

D. How many tens did you regroup as ones? _____ tens

How many ones did you put in each group? _____ one

E. Fran can put _____ stickers in each scrapbook.

Turn and Talk Where should you write the first digit of the whole-number quotient for the division 3)‾423 ?

2 Randall has 252 soccer badges. He puts the same number of badges into 4 scrapbooks. How many badges are in each scrapbook?

Use base-ten blocks to show 252 ÷ 4.

A. Were there enough hundreds to put at least 1 in each group? Why or why not?

_____

B. Where should you write the first digit in the

whole-number quotient? _____

C. What did you do with the 2 hundreds so they could be equally divided among 4 groups?

_____

D. How many tens did you put in each group? _____

E. Did you regroup any tens as ones? Why?

_____

F. How many ones did you put in each group? _____

G. There are _____ badges in each scrapbook.

Turn and Talk When you divide a 3-digit number by a 1-digit number, how many digits can the whole-number quotient have?

Step It Out

3 Now use long division to record each step as you use base-ten blocks to represent the division.

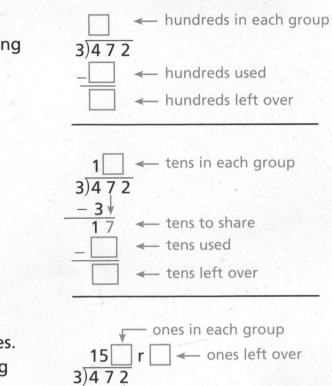

Find 472 ÷ 3.

A. Share the hundreds equally among the 3 groups.

_____ hundred is in each group.

_____ hundred is left over.

```
      □  ← hundreds in each group
  3)4 7 2
   -□    ← hundreds used
    □    ← hundreds left over
```

B. Regroup the leftover hundred as tens. Share all the tens equally among the 3 groups.

_____ tens are in each group.

_____ tens are left over.

```
    1□    ← tens in each group
  3)4 7 2
   - 3↓
    1 7   ← tens to share
   -□     ← tens used
    □     ← tens left over
```

C. Regroup the leftover tens as ones. Share all the ones equally among the 3 groups.

_____ ones are in each group.

_____ one is left over.

```
            ← ones in each group
    15□ r □ ← ones left over
  3)4 7 2
   -3
    1 7
   -1 5↓
      2 2  ← ones to share
     -□    ← ones used
      □    ← ones left over
```

D. Write the whole-number quotient and remainder for 472 ÷ 3. _____ r_____

• •

Check Understanding [Math Board]

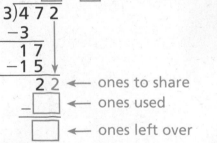

1 Terri saves $375 for a 4-day vacation. Does she have enough to spend $100 each day? How do you know?

_____

_____

On Your Own

MP Use Tools Use base-ten blocks to represent the division. Then record the results.

2 Athena uses this entire box of building blocks to build 2 identical towers. How many blocks does Athena use for each tower?

BUILDING BLOCKS

388 Pieces

_____

3 Jackie places 552 photos of cats on 4 bulletin boards at the animal shelter. Each board has the same number of photos. How many photos are on each board?

_____

MP Reason Tell how many digits in the whole-number quotient.

4 198 ÷ 3

5 351 ÷ 2

6 182 ÷ 4

_____   _____   _____

MP Reason Tell where to write the first digit in the whole-number quotient.

7 6)724

8 2)152

9 9)832

_____   _____   _____

10 Open Ended Write two division problems with a 1-digit divisor and a 3-digit dividend. One problem should have a 2-digit whole-number quotient. The other should have a 3-digit whole-number quotient. Explain how you chose your numbers.

_____

_____

_____

On Your Own

11 (MP) **Critique Reasoning** Mara completes this division. Is her answer correct? Why or why not?

```
        8 2 0 r3
    5)4 1 3
     -4 0
        1 3
       -1 0
           3
```

_____

_____

_____

12 (MP) **Attend to Precision** Ricardo has 325 tiles to make 4 mosaics. He uses the same number of tiles for each mosaic. How many tiles does Ricardo use for each mosaic? How many tiles does he have left over?

_____

Divide.

13 3)525

14 7)852

15 6)138

© Houghton Mifflin Harcourt Publishing Company

⬡ I'm in a Learning Mindset!

How did using base-ten blocks help me understand where to write the first digit in a whole-number quotient?

_____

_____

Name
_____

Divide by 1-Digit Numbers

(**I Can**) divide a multi-digit number by a 1-digit number and check the answer.

Step It Out

1 Jenni has 4,155 tickets for the air show. She gives the same number of tickets to 4 schools in the area. How many tickets does each school get?

A. Divide the thousands.

- _____ thousand is in each group.

- Subtract the _____ thousands in groups.

- There are 0 leftover thousands to regroup.

B. Divide the hundreds.

- You cannot share 1 hundred among 4 groups. So, write a **0** in the hundreds place of the whole-number quotient.

- Regroup the 1 hundred as _____ tens.

C. Divide the tens.

- _____ tens are in each group.

- Subtract the _____ tens in groups.

- Regroup the _____ leftover tens.

D. Divide the ones.

- _____ ones are in each group.

- Subtract the _____ ones in groups.

- Write the _____ leftover ones as the remainder.

E. Each school gets _____ tickets.

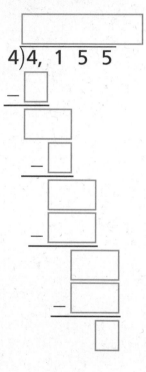

Step It Out

2 Division and multiplication are inverse operations. So, you can use multiplication to check your answer to a division problem.

A. Show the relationship between multiplication and division when there is no remainder.

Dividend ÷ Divisor = Quotient

Quotient × _____ = _____

B. Show the relationship when there is a remainder.

Whole-Number Quotient × _____ + _____ = _____

C. Apply the relationships to check division.

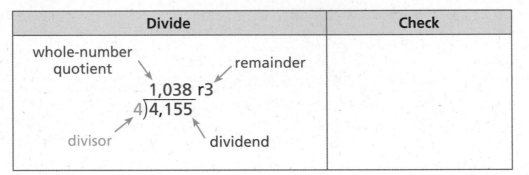

Divide	Check
whole-number quotient → 1,038 r3 ← remainder 4)4,155 divisor → ← dividend	

 Turn and Talk What are other ways you can check that your answer to a division problem is reasonable?

Check Understanding   `Math Board`

Divide and check.

1 2)3,471

2 5)5,145

On Your Own

3 (MP) **Reason** A single-engine airplane with fuel can carry a maximum of 460 pounds in cargo. The pilot wants to load 5 boxes of equipment. If all the boxes have the same weight, what is the maximum weight each box can have?

(MP) **Attend to Precision** Divide and check.

4 3)458

5 8)8,141

6 4)3,448

7 6)6,259

8 (MP) **Use Structure** When you divide a 4-digit number by a 1-digit number, how many digits can the whole-number quotient have? Explain how you know.

On Your Own

9 **STEM** The force of wind can change how fast an airplane flies. With a tailwind, a plane flies 2,340 miles in 5 hours. With a headwind, the plane flies the same distance in 6 hours. If the plane with the headwind flies the same distance every hour, how many miles does it fly each hour?

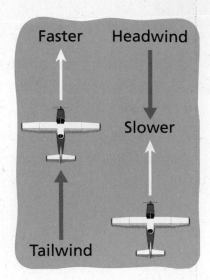

Faster   Headwind

Slower

Tailwind

10 **(MP)** **Attend to Precision** Mr. Tyler buys 4 round-trip tickets from Ft. Lauderdale, Florida, to Toronto, Canada. The total cost is $2,156. How much does each ticket cost?

11 **Open Ended** Write and solve a story problem that can be modeled by the equation **7,568 ÷ 7 = n.**

12 **(MP)** **Critique Reasoning** Delton completes this division. Is his answer correct? Explain why or why not.

```
        1 4 2 r2
  3)3,1 2 8
  − 3
    0 1 2
    − 1 2
        0 8
      −   6
          2
```

Name

Solve Multistep Multiplication and Division Problems

(I Can) solve multistep word problems involving multiplication, division, and interpretation of remainders.

Step It Out

1 Four classes participate in the first Field Day session. Each class has 21 students. They play in 3 teams with the same number of students on each team. How many students are on each team?

A. Think about the first step. How can you find the total number of students?

_____

B. Think about the second step. How can you find the number of students on each team?

_____

C. Draw a visual model and write an equation to represent each step.

D. Use the visual model and equations to solve the problem. _____ students are on each team.

 Turn and Talk How do you know that your answer is reasonable?

Step It Out

2 Remi has 3 batches of photos from Field Day. Each batch has 19 photos. She puts 4 photos on each page of her album. How many album pages does Remi use?

A. Think about the first step. Why can you multiply to find the total number of photos?

_____

B. Think about the second step. Why can you divide to find the number of album pages Remi uses?

_____

C. Write equations to model each step.

Number of photos, _n_: _____

Number of pages, _p_: _____

D. Use the equations to solve the problem.

Remi uses _____ album pages.

 Turn and Talk How did the remainder affect your answer to the question in this problem?

• •

Check Understanding [Math Board]

1 There are 48 people going on a hike. Each pack of water has 8 bottles.

• How many packs are needed for each hiker to have 2 bottles?

_____

• How can you check that your answer is reasonable?

_____

On Your Own

2 (MP) **Attend to Precision** A chef has 5 dozen eggs. How many 3-egg omelets can the chef make?

1 dozen

3 (MP) **Model with Mathematics** Juan buys 10 bottles of juice for a party. Each bottle holds 24 fluid ounces. How many 6-fluid ounce glasses can Juan fill with the juice? Write equations to model and solve the problem. Use z for the number of fluid ounces and g for the number of glasses.

4 (MP) **Reason** The manager of a basketball league buys 96 practice jerseys for 6 teams. Each team has 8 players, and each player gets the same number of jerseys. How many practice jerseys does each player get?

5 (MP) **Reason** Four friends buy 3 packages of these erasers. They share the erasers equally among themselves and give any leftover erasers to their teacher. How many erasers do they give to the teacher?

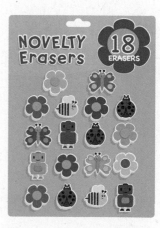

NOVELTY Erasers 18 ERASERS

On Your Own

6 (MP) **Attend to Precision** Mr. Drake buys tickets for a movie at the museum. He buys tickets for himself and his wife and for his children and their friends. The total is $46. How many child tickets does Mr. Drake buy?

MUSEUM
MOVIE
THEATER

Adult: $7.00

Child: $4.00

_____

7 (MP) **Attend to Precision** There are 90 students in the fourth grade. They are divided into 3 equal classes. Each class is separated into teams of 6 students. How many teams are in each fourth-grade class?

_____

8 (MP) **Reason** Simon has 2 boxes of car models. Each box has 23 models. He displays the models on shelves that can hold 8 models each. What is the least number of shelves he needs for all the models? How do you know?

_____

_____

9 (MP) **Construct Arguments** Anita plans a party for 96 guests. She can rent all rectangular or all round tables. Which kind of table should she rent? Explain your choice.

Table Rentals		
Table Size	Seats	Price
5-ft rectangle	6	$8
5-ft round	8	$9

_____

_____

© Houghton Mifflin Harcourt Publishing Company

Concepts and Skills

1 What division problem and answer does this quick picture represent? How do you know?

_____

_____

_____

(MP) **Use Tools** Divide. Name the strategy or tool you will use to solve the problem, explain your choice, and then find the answer.

2 72 ÷ 6 _____   **3** 95 ÷ 8 _____   **4** 32 ÷ 7 _____

_____

_____

_____

5 Luann uses 356 beads to decorate 4 picture frames. She uses the same number of beads on each frame. How many beads does Luann use for each frame?

(A) 87   (C) 89

(B) 90   (D) 86

Divide and check.

6 $5\overline{)231}$ **7** $3\overline{)458}$ **8** $8\overline{)165}$

9 $4\overline{)3,944}$ **10** $6\overline{)6,259}$ **11** $7\overline{)2,551}$

12 Which statements about the division problem are true?
Select all the correct answers.

$8\overline{)4,568}$

Ⓐ The first digit of the whole-number quotient is in the thousands place.

Ⓑ There is no remainder.

Ⓒ You need to regroup thousands as hundreds to divide.

Ⓓ The whole-number quotient has three digits.

Ⓔ You need to write a 0 in the whole-number quotient.

13 A baker makes 8 dozen muffins. She puts 5 muffins in each box to sell. How many boxes can she fill? (1 dozen = 12)

Extend and Apply Multiplication

Urban Planner

Did you ever notice how cities and towns are organized into different areas for stores, homes, parks, and schools? That's the work of an urban planner!

In 1791, George Washington hired Pierre L'Enfant to plan the city of Washington, D.C. L'Enfant's blueprint included avenues leading to the Capitol building with squares, circles, and triangles at street intersections for monuments and fountains. When L'Enfant quit and took the city plans with him, Benjamin Banneker rose to the challenge. Banneker saved the project by drawing, from memory, a layout of the city's streets, parks, and buildings.

STEM Task:

Urban planners must consider the impact of their plans on wildlife and water quality. They plan recreation areas and parks. Discuss with classmates what is important to include in a community. With your group draw a shape on a piece of paper to represent your community. Decide on a name. Then work together to draw and label areas for the things you decided are important.

People progress at different rates. Urban planners who are good at one thing may seek a new job that challenges them in new ways. For example, a planner who is skilled at energy and water infrastructure may still be learning about traffic patterns. How we approach challenges goes a long way to determining our success. In math, you may learn one concept quickly and easily, but struggle with another. Try to define the things that you need to do, without comparing yourself to others. By defining your own challenges, you can keep your focus on your own work and progress.

Reflect

Q Was the STEM task challenging for you? Explain why or why not.

Q What type of activity would have been a better challenge for you?

Multiply by 2-Digit Numbers

Do I have enough rope?

- There is a school track meet today and your job is to make sure fans stay off of the track. To do this, you will have to tie pieces of rope together to make a rope that is long enough to go around the track.

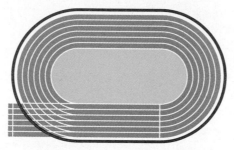

Distance around outside of track: 440 meters

- Which will be enough rope to go around the track?

  A. 44 pieces of rope that are each 10 meters long

  B. 8 pieces of rope that are each 60 meters long

  C. 6 pieces of rope that are each 70 meters long

  D. 5 pieces of rope that are each 80 meters long

 Turn and Talk

- Do you need more or less than 440 meters of rope?

- How can you solve the problem?

Are You Ready?

Complete these problems to review prior concepts and skills
you will need for this module.

Multiplication Facts Through 10

Use the different strategies to find the product.

1 Draw an array to find 4 × 6.

I drew _____ rows of _____ tiles.

There are _____ tiles.

4 × 6 = _____

2 Use a number line to find 3 × 4.

I drew _____ jumps of _____
spaces each.

0 1 2 3 4 5 6 7 8 9 10 11 12 13 14 15 16

The last jump ends at _____.

3 × 4 = _____

Multiplication Facts

Find the product.

3 4 × 7

_____

4 7 × 6

_____

5 9 × 5

_____

Multiples of 10, 100, and 1,000

Find the product.

6 3 × 1 = _____

3 × 10 = _____

3 × 100 = _____

3 × 1,000 = _____

7 9 × 5 = _____

9 × 50 = _____

9 × 500 = _____

9 × 5,000 = _____

8 6 × 3 = _____

6 × 30 = _____

6 × 300 = _____

6 × 3,000 = _____

Name _____

Multiply with Tens

(**I Can**) use different strategies to multiply with multiples of ten.

Spark Your Learning

The coding club uses a coding website that has 20 projects. Each project takes 24 steps to complete. During a session, the club will complete all of the projects. What multiplication strategy can you use to find out how many steps the club will work through?

Show your thinking.

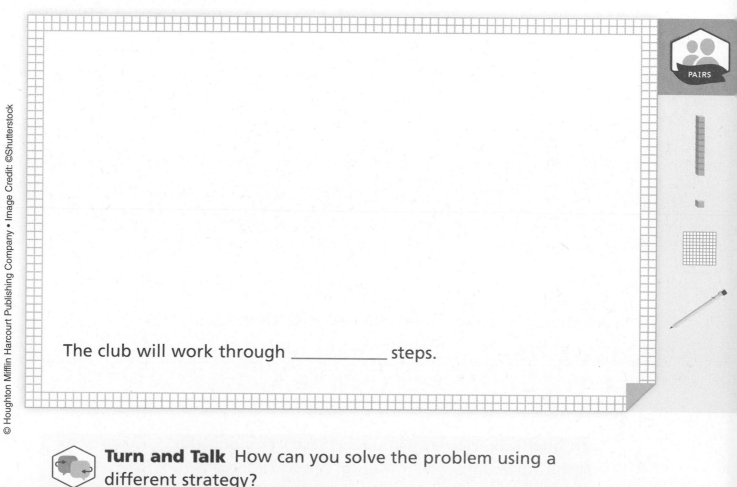

The club will work through _____ steps.

Turn and Talk How can you solve the problem using a different strategy?

Build Understanding

1 The coding club meets for 60 minutes each week for 16 weeks. How many minutes will they meet during the 16-week period?

A. How can you rename one of the factors using place value?

_____

Show how you can use place value to find the product.

The coding club meets for _____ minutes during the 16 weeks.

B. How did using place value help you to solve the problem?

_____

_____

Turn and Talk How can you use place value and the Commutative Property of Multiplication to solve a multiplication problem that has a ten?

2 It takes 12 lines of code to move a character through an obstacle course. Adrian wants to move 30 characters through the course. How many lines of code will she write?

How can you find 30 × 12 using different methods?

A. Use the Associative Property of Multiplication.

- How can you rename one of the factors as a product of a number and 10?

  _____

- 30 × 12 = (_____ × _____) × 12 What is another way to think of 30?

- How can you use the Associative Property of Multiplication to solve?

  _____

B. Use halving and doubling to find the product.

- Of which factor can you find half to make the problem simpler? Why?

  _____

- _____ × _____ = _____ What is the product of the half and the other factor?

- You found half of the product. What can you do to find the final product?

  _____

  _____

C. Adrian will write _____ lines of code.

· ·

Check Understanding

Choose a method to solve the problem.

1 How many paper clips are in 20 boxes?

_____

On Your Own

2 (MP) **Reason** Eva puts 70 rubber bands of each color in the container. She says she has 1,470 rubber bands. What strategy will you use to determine if she is correct? Why?

_____

_____

_____

3 **Open Ended** Show how you can find the product 15 × 90 in your own way.

4 **STEM** Millions of documents, thousands of hours of music, and as many as 25,000 photos can be stored on a 64-gigabyte flash drive. How many gigabytes of data can be stored on 20 flash drives of this size?

_____

Choose a method. Then find the product.

5 80 × 29 = _____ **6** 35 × 30 = _____ **7** 90 × 16 = _____

➖✖️➕➗ I'm in a Learning Mindset!

What challenges did you face in this lesson?

_____

_____

Name _____

Estimate Products

(**I Can**) estimate products using a variety of methods and predict how the estimated product will relate to the actual product.

Spark Your Learning

Mr. Adkins has this problem on the board for morning work. Use the problem to answer the following questions:

What might the unknown numbers be?

How many different answers can you find?

Show your thinking.

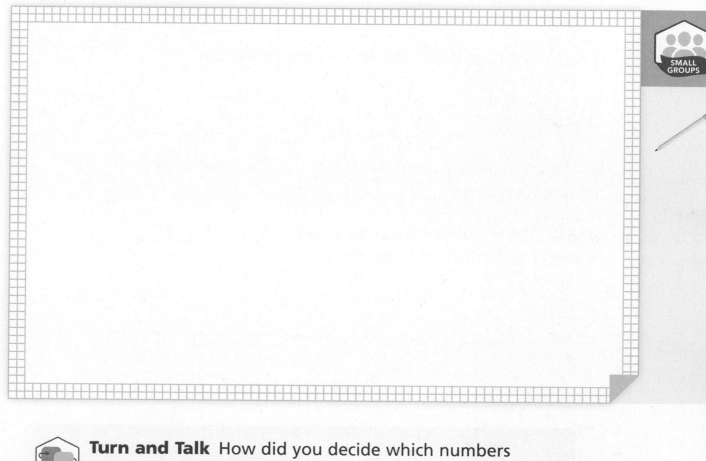

□ × □ is about 250.

Turn and Talk How did you decide which numbers might solve the problem?

Build Understanding

1 For all of the fourth-grade science centers, Mr. Adkins made 11 discovery boxes with 23 small objects in each box. About how many objects did he have to gather for the discovery boxes?

A. What is an estimate?

_____

_____

B. How can you use rounding to determine a reasonable estimate for the number of objects Mr. Adkins gathered?

_____

_____

C. How can you use basic facts to find the estimate?

_____

_____

D. Mr. Adkins had to gather about _____ objects for the discovery boxes.

E. How do the rounded numbers compare to the factors? How will this affect your estimate?

_____

_____

_____

Turn and Talk How can an overestimate and an underestimate affect a real-life situation?

Step It Out

2 ▶ Mr. Adkins challenges his students to spend 45 minutes without electronics on each school day in November. For about how many minutes will each student be electronics-free in November?

November						
Sunday	Monday	Tuesday	Wednesday	Thursday	Friday	Saturday
			1	2	3	4
5	6	7	8	9	10	11
12	13	14	15	16	17	18
19	20	21	No School		25
26	27	28	29	30		

Use front-end estimation to estimate the product.

A. In what place value is the front digit in each number? _____

B. Circle the tens. Then write the estimated factors changing all of the other digits to zero.

   1 9   4 5
   ↓   ↓

   _____   _____

C. Find the product of the estimated factors.

   _____ × _____ = _____

Use rounding to estimate the same product.

D. Round each factor to the nearest ten.

   _____ × _____

E. Find the product of the rounded factors.

   _____ × _____ = _____

F. Compare the estimates. Which estimate is more reasonable? Why?

   _____

   _____

G. Each student will be electronics-free for about _____ minutes in November.

Turn and Talk Why can there be more than one estimate for any problem?

191

Step It Out

3 Mr. Adkin's students each make 8 origami animals. There are 27 students in his class. How can you use compatible numbers to estimate the number of origami animals the students make?

A. Write compatible numbers for 27 and 8.

$$27 \quad \times \quad 8$$
$$\downarrow \qquad \qquad \downarrow$$
$$\underline{\hspace{3em}} \times \underline{\hspace{3em}}$$

> **Connect to Vocabulary**
>
> **Compatible numbers** are numbers that are easy to compute mentally.

B. Find the product of the compatible numbers.

$$\underline{\hspace{3em}} \times \underline{\hspace{3em}} = \underline{\hspace{3em}}$$

C. The students make about _____ origami animals.

D. How will this estimate compare with the actual product? How do you know?

_____

_____

. . . .

Check Understanding [Math Board]

Estimate the product 37 × 24 using each method.

1 front-end estimation   **2** rounding   **3** compatible numbers

_____   _____   _____

4 Which method for estimating would be most reasonable if you wanted to make sure you had 37 craft materials for each of the 24 students in art class? Why?

_____

_____

On Your Own

5 (MP) **Use Structure** Mrs. Hernandez is shopping for a new cell phone plan. She knows that she sends about 28 texts each day. The greatest number of days in any month is 31. How can she use estimation to help her decide which cell phone plan would be best for her?

Type of Cell Phone Plan	Number of Texts per Month
Basic	600
Extra	800
Supreme	1,000

_____

_____

_____

6 (MP) **Reason** Bella decides to read for 45 minutes each day for 22 days. What is an estimate for the number of minutes Bella will read?

_____

_____

7 (MP) **Critique Reasoning** Ian wants to save $425 to buy a new video game system. He earns $15 each week for chores he does around his home. He estimates that if he saves his money for 24 weeks, he will have enough to buy the game system. Do you agree with Ian? Why or why not?

_____

_____

Estimate the product. Choose a method.

8 86×43

9 32×71

10 $33 \times \$46$

_____

_____

_____

11 11×27

12 $\$72 \times 25$

13 56×65

_____

_____

_____

On Your Own

14 (MP) **Reason** A local bakery needs muffin wrappers for 28 batches of muffins. There are 24 muffins in each batch. About how many muffin wrappers will the bakery need? Explain how you can estimate to solve the problem.

_____

_____

_____

15 Melinda quickly enters 49×13 into her calculator. The display shows a product. How can Melinda use estimation to check that this product is correct?

_____

_____

_____

Estimate the product. Choose a method.

16 86×42

17 31×23

18 78×77

_____   _____   _____

19 91×15

20 25×51

21 68×41

_____   _____   _____

⬡ I'm in a Learning Mindset!

What did I learn from estimating products that I can use in the future?

_____

_____

Name _____

Relate Area Models and Partial Products

(I Can) use area models and partial products to multiply two 2-digit numbers.

Spark Your Learning

A stained glass artist explains that the purpose of stained glass windows is to control light or tell a story. They contain pieces of colorful glass arranged in patterns or pictures held together in a form by strips of lead. How many different multiplication problems can you write using the measures of these glass pieces?

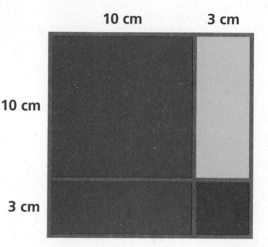

Turn and Talk How did you decide on the factors for each multiplication problem?

Build Understanding

1 In Dr. Brewer's art class, students will be making 15 rag rugs. Each rug uses 14 yards of fabric. How many yards of fabric will be needed to make all of the rag rugs?

A. How can you find the number of yards of fabric needed?

_____

_____

B. Show how you can use an area model to represent the problem.

_____ × _____ = _____

_____ × _____ = _____

_____ × _____ = _____

_____ × _____ = _____

C. How can you write multiplication equations to find the partial products? Record the equations above.

D. How can you use the partial products to find the whole product?

_____

E. _____ yards of fabric will be needed to make the rag rugs.

 Turn and Talk How does the area model make it easier to find the product?

Step It Out

2 In the storage closet, there are 17 different types of paint brushes with 23 of each type. How many paint brushes are there?

A. Break apart each factor into tens and ones.

$17 =$ _____ + _____

$23 =$ _____ + _____

B. Label the area model with the factors.

C. Use the Distributive Property to find the partial products.

20 _____

10

_____

$(10 \times 20) + ($ _____ $\times$ _____ $) + ($ _____ $\times$ _____ $) + ($ _____ $\times$ _____ $)$

10×2 tens 10×3 ones 7×2 tens 7×3 ones

D. Add the partial products to find the whole product.

_____ + _____ + _____ + _____ = _____

E. There are _____ paint brushes in the storage closet.

Turn and Talk How does the area model show that the sum of the partial products is the product?

Check Understanding [Math Board]

Complete the area model. Find the product.

1 $13 \times 16 =$ _____

10 _____

10

On Your Own

2 (MP) **Model with Mathematics** Complete the area model. Write and solve an equation for the area model.

_____ × _____ = _____

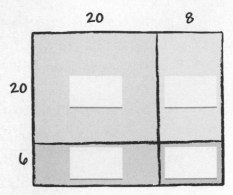

3 (MP) **Reason** There are 22 students in Mrs. Taylor's fourth grade class. Each student is asked to bring in 15 pencils at the beginning of the school year. How can you determine how many pencils the class will have as the new school year begins?

_____

_____

Draw an area model to represent the product. Then record the product.

4 17 × 13 = _____

5 14 × 21 = _____

I'm in a Learning Mindset!

How did practice help me master area models and partial products?

_____

Name _____

Multiply Using Partial Products

(I Can) multiply two 2-digit numbers using different methods.

Step It Out

1 Oranges grow on trees in a group, with very little undergrowth, called a grove. A section of an orange grove has 32 rows with 24 trees in a row. How many orange trees are in the section?

Multiply. 32 × 24

A. Find and record the partial products. Line up the partial products by place value.

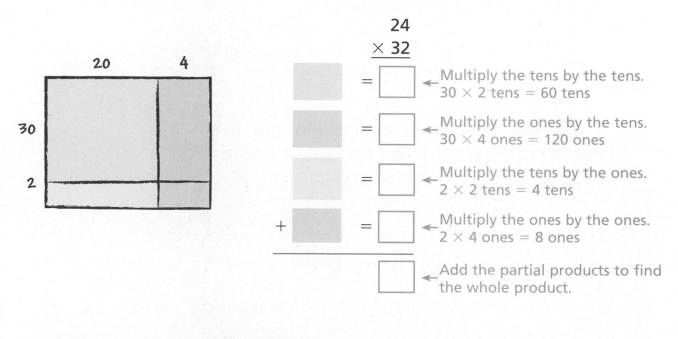

$$\begin{array}{r} 24 \\ \times\ 32 \end{array}$$

☐ = ☐ ← Multiply the tens by the tens.
30 × 2 tens = 60 tens

☐ = ☐ ← Multiply the ones by the tens.
30 × 4 ones = 120 ones

☐ = ☐ ← Multiply the tens by the ones.
2 × 2 tens = 4 tens

+ ☐ = ☐ ← Multiply the ones by the ones.
2 × 4 ones = 8 ones

☐ ← Add the partial products to find the whole product.

B. There are _____ orange trees in the section.

Turn and Talk Why is it important to align the partial products by place value?

Step It Out

2 Oranges are often packaged in crates so that they can be shipped to different places. How many oranges are packed in 62 crates to be shipped?

contains 48 oranges

A. Multiply. _____ × _____   **Estimate.** _____

$$\boxed{}$$
$$\underline{\times\ 62}$$

B. Multiply the tens by the tens. $\boxed{}$ ← 60 × _____ tens = _____ tens

C. Multiply the ones by the tens. $\boxed{}$ ← 60 × _____ ones = _____ ones

D. Multiply the tens by the ones. $\boxed{}$ ← 2 × _____ tens = _____ tens

E. Multiply the ones by the ones. $+\ \boxed{}$ ← 2 × _____ ones = _____ ones

F. Add the partial products to find the whole product. $\boxed{}$ oranges

  Turn and Talk How does the product compare with your estimate? How does the comparison help you to determine if your answer is reasonable?

- -

Check Understanding Math Board

Estimate. Then use partial products to find the product.

1 Estimate: _____

$$35$$
$$\underline{\times\ 47}$$

2 Estimate: _____

$$89$$
$$\underline{\times\ 67}$$

On Your Own

3 There are 87 seats available for a concert. Each ticket costs the same amount. How much would all of the tickets cost for the

available seats? _____

STALLS: G43 **$55**
SECTION: GREEN

THE HMH ARENA
PRESENTS
ROCK BAND

DOORS OPEN: 18:30
DATE: MAY 29

THIS TICKET MUST BE RETAINED

4 Mr. Edgar works 38 hours each week for 49 weeks every year. How many hours does

he work in a year? _____

(MP) Use Structure **Estimate. Then use partial products to find the product.**

5 Estimate: _____

$$\begin{array}{r} 29 \\ \times\ 53 \\ \hline \end{array}$$

6 Estimate: _____

$$\begin{array}{r} 61 \\ \times\ 19 \\ \hline \end{array}$$

7 Estimate: _____

$$\begin{array}{r} 14 \\ \times\ 79 \\ \hline \end{array}$$

8 Estimate: _____

$$\begin{array}{r} 92 \\ \times\ 38 \\ \hline \end{array}$$

9 Estimate: _____

$$\begin{array}{r} 46 \\ \times\ 58 \\ \hline \end{array}$$

10 Estimate: _____

$$\begin{array}{r} 85 \\ \times\ 76 \\ \hline \end{array}$$

11 (MP) **Use Repeated Reasoning** How can you use the product 2×54 to find the product 22×54?

_____

_____

_____

12 (MP) **Model with Mathematics** There are 52 cards in a deck of fact cards. How many cards are in 36 decks? Write an equation and solve.

_____

Rewrite the problem. Then use partial products to find the product.

13 $65 \times 33 =$ _____

14 $21 \times 42 =$ _____

15 $24 \times 84 =$ _____

16 $97 \times 56 =$ _____

Name _____

Multiply with Regrouping

(I Can) fluently multiply two 2-digit numbers using the method of regrouping.

Step It Out

1 A music store has 12 standard pianos on display. A standard piano has 88 keys. How many piano keys are in the display at the music store?

Multiply. _____ × _____

Estimate. _____

A. Write the problem vertically. Then use place value and regrouping to find the answer.

B. Where did you need to regroup? Why?

_____

_____

_____

_____

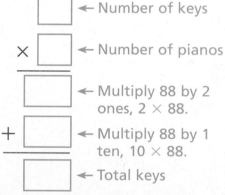

← Number of keys

× ← Number of pianos

← Multiply 88 by 2 ones, 2 × 88.

+ ← Multiply 88 by 1 ten, 10 × 88.

← Total keys

C. Why did you record a zero in the ones place of the second partial product?

_____

_____

_____

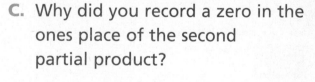 **Turn and Talk** How do you know if your answer is reasonable?

Step It Out

2 Mrs. Singh is making a booklet of guitar music that contains 76 pages. She will need 27 copies of the booklet for her class. How many sheets of paper will she use to make the booklets?

Multiply. _____ × _____

Estimate. _____

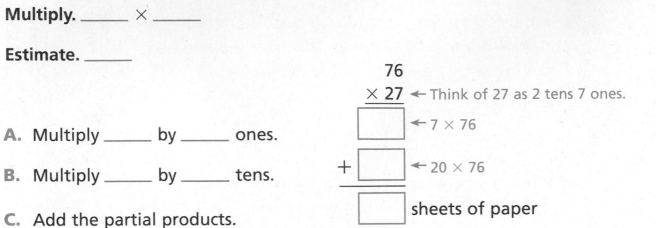

```
      76
   ×  27  ← Think of 27 as 2 tens 7 ones.
   ┌────┐
   │    │  ← 7 × 76
   └────┘
  ┌────┐
+ │    │  ← 20 × 76
  └────┘
   ┌────┐
   │    │  sheets of paper
   └────┘
```

A. Multiply _____ by _____ ones.

B. Multiply _____ by _____ tens.

C. Add the partial products.

D. How can you check to see if the product is reasonable?

_____

_____

Turn and Talk How can you use regrouping to multiply?

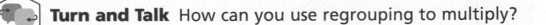

Check Understanding [Math Board]

Estimate. Then find the product.

1 Estimate: _____
```
    88
  × 63
```

2 Estimate: _____
```
    94
  × 18
```

3 Estimate: _____
```
    23
  × 16
```

Name: _____

On Your Own

4 (MP) **Reason** David wrote that the product of 69 and 52 is 4,318. Is his answer reasonable? Explain.

_____

_____

_____

5 Angelina is training for an ultra marathon. She will run a total of 22 miles a week for 28 weeks. How many miles will Angelina run? _____

Estimate. Then find the product.

6 Estimate: _____
64
× 28

7 Estimate: _____
66
× 79

8 Estimate: _____
89
× 49

9 Estimate: _____
73
× 84

10 Estimate: _____
55
× 39

11 Estimate: _____
94
× 56

12 Twelve parents signed up to make 24 muffins each for the fifth-grade tea. How many muffins will there be for the tea?

_____

13 **Music** A harp is an instrument with 47 strings that run down at an angle to a soundboard. If a company builds 39 harps in a year, how many strings will they use?

_____

Estimate. Then find the product.

14 Estimate: _____

34
× 31

15 Estimate: _____

89
× 27

16 Estimate: _____

56
× 71

17 Estimate: _____

48
× 19

18 Estimate: _____

32
× 64

19 Estimate: _____

96
× 82

20 (MP) **Construct Arguments** Eli makes 28 decorative bookmarks for his classmates. It takes 75 centimeters of yarn to make each bookmark. How much yarn does Eli use? Explain how you used regrouping to solve the problem.

_____

_____

_____

_____

Name _____

Choose a Multiplication Strategy

(**I Can**) fluently multiply two 2-digit numbers using the method of my choice.

Step It Out

1 Most professional soccer matches require 14 soccer balls. The traditional soccer ball has 32 panels, each representing one country in Europe. How can you multiply using partial products to find out how many panels are on 14 traditional soccer balls?

Multiply: _____ × _____

Estimate: _____

$$\begin{array}{r} 32 \\ \times\ 14 \\ \end{array}$$

A. Multiply 3 tens by 10 = _____ tens = ☐

B. Multiply 2 ones by 10 = _____ tens = ☐

C. Multiply 3 tens by 4 = _____ ones = ☐

D. Multiply 2 ones by 4 = _____ ones = + ☐

E. Add the partial products. ☐ panels

F. How do you know if your answer is reasonable?

_____

_____

_____

Turn and Talk How can you use the Distributive Property to solve the problem?

Step It Out

2 At the beginning of each season, the National Basketball Association sends each of the 29 American teams 72 basketballs. How can you multiply with regrouping to find out how many basketballs are sent?

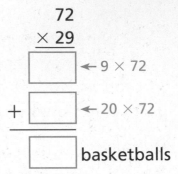

Multiply. _____ × _____

Estimate. _____

A. Multiply _____ by _____ ones.

B. Multiply _____ by _____ tens.

C. Add the partial products.

D. How do you know if your answer is reasonable?

_____

_____

_____

$$
\begin{array}{r}
72 \\
\times\ 29 \\
\hline
\boxed{} \leftarrow 9 \times 72 \\
+\ \boxed{} \leftarrow 20 \times 72 \\
\hline
\boxed{}\ \text{basketballs}
\end{array}
$$

Check Understanding [Math Board]

1 For each Championship Bowl, 76 footballs are used. How many footballs have been used in 52 Championship Bowls?

_____

Estimate. Then choose a method to find the product.

2 Estimate: _____

$$
\begin{array}{r}
37 \\
\times\ 26 \\
\hline
\end{array}
$$

3 Estimate: _____

$$
\begin{array}{r}
82 \\
\times\ 49 \\
\hline
\end{array}
$$

4 Estimate: _____

$$
\begin{array}{r}
91 \\
\times\ 77 \\
\hline
\end{array}
$$

On Your Own

5 (MP) **Model with Mathematics** A bag of frozen strawberries contains 91 strawberries. How many strawberries are in 76 bags?

A. Use partial products to find the product.

76 × 91 = _____

B. Draw a picture to check your work.

Estimate. Then choose a method to find the product.

6 Estimate: _____

43
× 35
‾‾‾‾

7 Estimate: _____

59
× 18
‾‾‾‾

8 Estimate: _____

86
× 72
‾‾‾‾

9 Josie picks 13 berries from each of 23 blueberry bushes. How many berries does she pick?

_____

10 (MP) **Use Repeated Reasoning** Why is the second partial product greater than the first partial product when you multiply two 2-digit numbers with regrouping?

_____

_____

_____

_____

On Your Own

11 (MP) **Construct Arguments** A scientific calculator has 54 keys. There are 68 of that type of scientific calculator in the resource room. Gina wondered how many keys that is.

- Use partial products to find the product.

    $54 \times 68 =$ _____

- Use the Distributive Property to check your work.

12 (MP) **Reason** An order was placed for new flags for the color guard. The flags cost $34 each. If the color guard director pays for 16 flags with six $100 bills, how much change will the director receive? How did you find the answer?

_____

_____

Find the unknown digits. Complete the problem.

13

```
        7 □
    ×   3 3
    ─────────
    2 2 8
+ 2, □ 8 0
─────────
  2, 5 0 8
```

14

```
      5 9
  ×   4 □
  ─────────
      5 9
+ □, 3 6 0
─────────
  □, 4 1 9
```

15

```
          8 5
    ×   □ 5
  ─────────────
  □ □ □
+ 5, 1 0 0
─────────────
  5, 5 □ □
```

16 (MP) **Construct Arguments** How do you know which of the following costs more, 38 sweaters at $49 each or 48 pairs of

jeans at $39 each? _____

_____

Name _____

Solve Multistep Problems and Assess Reasonableness

(I Can) solve word problems that involve two and three steps using whole numbers and all four operations.

Step It Out

1   Mr. Azqui designed a mural that will cover 340 square meters of an old factory wall. He and some volunteers have collected 13 gallons of paint to complete the mural. Each gallon of paint will cover 37 square meters. Is there enough paint to fill the mural? If so, how many additional square meters could be painted?

A. What do you need to find?

_____

B. Underline the information that you need to solve the problem.

C. How can you solve the problem?

_____

_____

_____

_____

D. Solve the problem. What did you find?

_____

_____

Turn and Talk How can you check if your answer is reasonable?

Step It Out

2 At Hansel's Orchard 48 apples can fit in a basket. One day, Mr. Kelvin and some friends pick enough apples to fill 28 baskets. It takes 8 apples to make a jar of applesauce. How many jars of applesauce can Mr. Kelvin make from these apples?

A. What information is given?

_____

_____

_____

B. How can you solve the problem?

_____

C. How many jars of applesauce can Mr. Kelvin make?

_____

D. How can you use estimation to check the reasonableness of your answer?

_____

_____

Check Understanding [Math Board]

1 Savannah earned money one summer by mowing lawns. She earned $23 for each of the 19 lawns she mowed. She earned $60 in tips. How much money did she earn? _____

2 A large box of dishwasher detergent costs $14. A new dishwasher costs 45 times that price. How much does a dishwasher and 3 boxes of detergent cost? _____

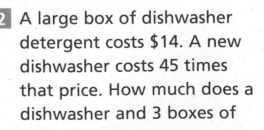

On Your Own

3 A middle school graduation is taking place in a theater with 2,817 seats. The school has 519 graduating students. Each student brings 4 guests. How many seats will be available for staff and teachers after the students and guests have been seated?

_____

4 (MP) **Reason** There are 23 adults on school buses for a field trip. There are 17 times as many students as adults on the field trip. If each of the 9 school buses used for the field trip have about the same number of students, how many students go on each bus? Interpret the problem and the remainder for this situation.

_____

_____

5 (MP) **Model with Mathematics** A loader uses a forklift to put 4 boxes that each weigh 158 pounds onto a truck. Then he loads 3 more boxes that each weigh 235 pounds onto the same truck. How many pounds of boxes did the loader put on the truck?

• Write an equation to model the situation and solve.

_____

• How can you check if your answer is reasonable?

_____

_____

6 **Open Ended** Write a word problem that can be modeled and solved using this equation: $34 \times 14 + 19 \times 11 = 685$.

_____

_____

On Your Own

7 A 5,000-seat stadium is having its seats repainted. So far, 6 sections with 236 seats and an additional 193 seats have been repainted. How many seats still

have to be repainted? _____

8 Manuela read a book that was 6 times longer than Jillian's 139-page book. Lydia read a book that was 292 pages shorter than Valerie's 834-page book. How many

pages did Manuela and Lydia read? _____

9 (MP) **Attend to Precision** A skyscraper has 62 floors. Of those floors, 58 have 39 offices and the other 4 floors have 26 offices.

- How many offices are in the skyscraper?

_____

- How can you check if your answer is reasonable?

_____

_____

_____

_____

10 An airplane flies from Los Angeles to Chicago and back every day. How many minutes is the plane in flight during a 7-day week?

_____

11 **Open Ended** Jenn writes 3 × 6 × 10 × 4 on the board. She asks if the answer is 560. How can you explain to Jenn whether or not the answer is 560?

_____

_____

Vocabulary

1 Write the correct term for the definition.
An example of this term is shown.

_____ are numbers
that are easy to compute mentally.

24×27
↓ ↓
25×30

Concepts and Skills

Estimate the product. Choose a method.

2 46×93

_____

3 23×17

_____

4 34×18

_____

5 89×21

_____

(MP) **Use Tools** Find the product. Name the strategy or
tool you will use to solve the problem, explain your
choice, and then find the answer.

6 $19 \times 60 =$ _____

7 $34 \times 60 =$ _____

8 $62 \times 30 =$ _____

9 $77 \times 40 =$ _____

_____

_____

_____

Estimate. Then choose a method to find the product.

10 Estimate: _____

$$\begin{array}{r} 32 \\ \times\ 47 \\ \hline \end{array}$$

11 Estimate: _____

$$\begin{array}{r} 76 \\ \times\ 29 \\ \hline \end{array}$$

12 Which unknown digits complete the problem?

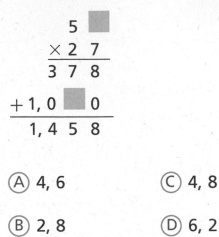

Ⓐ 4, 6   Ⓒ 4, 8

Ⓑ 2, 8   Ⓓ 6, 2

13 Vito is training for a race. He runs 14 miles a day for 16 days. Then he runs 10 miles a day for 3 days. How many fewer miles does he run the 3 days than the

16 days? _____

14 Draw an area model to represent the product. Then record the product.

21 × 37 = _____

Apply Multiplication to Area

What are some possible rectangles?

Kai is using a 64 foot rope to outline an area for a vegetable garden. Label the four rectangles with possible lengths and widths so that each rectangle has a perimeter of 64 feet.

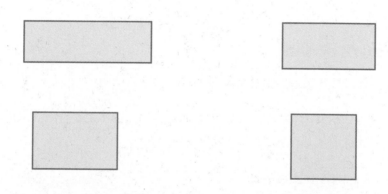

- What is the sum of the length and width of each of your rectangles?

_____

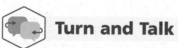 **Turn and Talk**

- What is the longest length that you could use if the measurements are only in whole feet? Explain.

- How did you decide the lengths and widths of the rectangles?

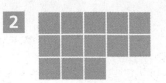

Are You Ready?

Complete these problems to review prior concepts and skills you will need for this module.

Explore Area

Count the unit squares to find the area of the figure.

1

The area of the figure is _____ square units.

2

The area of the figure is _____ square units.

Multiplication Facts

Use multiplication to solve the problem.

3 Mitch has 7 bags of marbles. Each bag contains 5 marbles. How many marbles does Mitch have?

Mitch has _____ marbles.

4 Mrs. Gonzalez receives 6 flowers from each of 9 students. How many flowers does Mrs. Gonzalez have?

Mrs. Gonzalez has _____ flowers.

Meaning of Multiplication: Arrays

Complete.

5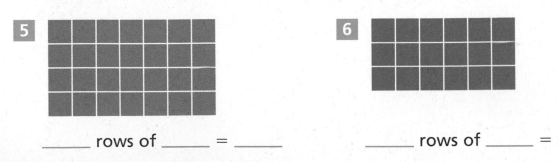

_____ rows of _____ = _____

6

_____ rows of _____ = _____

Name _____

Apply the Area Formula to Rectangles

(I Can) find the area of a rectangle by using the formula for area.

8 feet

STATE CHAMPIONS
Magnolia High
Girls
Soccer

5 feet

10 feet

STATE CHAMPIONS
Girls Soccer
Magnolia High School

4 feet

Spark Your Learning

Making banners is a very old craft. Banners are usually made of cloth and can have a symbol, logo, slogan, or any other message. How can you find the area of each banner?

Show your thinking.

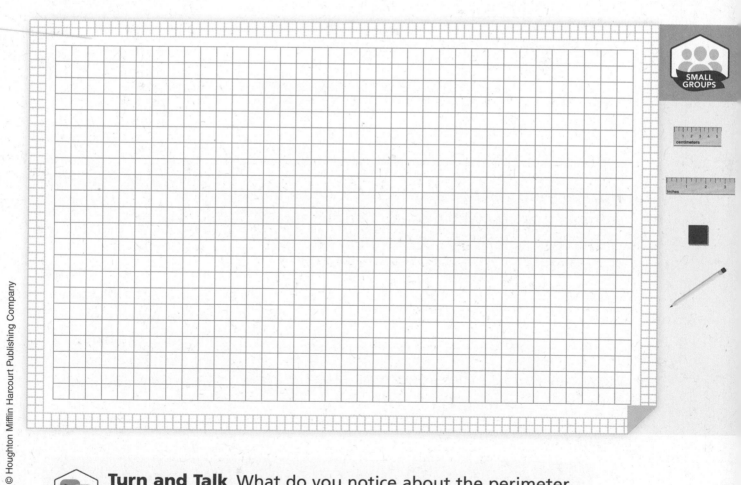

SMALL GROUPS

© Houghton Mifflin Harcourt Publishing Company

Turn and Talk What do you notice about the perimeter and area of each banner?

Build Understanding

1 Sports fans use banners to show support. How can you find the area of the banner?

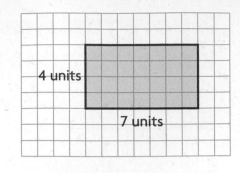

4 units

7 units

A. What does it mean to find the *area* of a flat surface?

_____

To find the area, think about the measure of the sides of the rectangle.

B. How many unit squares make up the length and width of the rectangle?

_____

C. Count the number of unit squares to find the area. _____

D. What is the relationship between the length and width

and the area? _____

_____

E. How can you describe a mathematical rule or formula that you would use to find the area (A) of the rectangle? Write the formula. Represent the length with l and the width with w.

_____

_____

F. How can you use the area formula to find the area of the rectangle?

$A = l \times w$

$A = \underline{\quad} \times \underline{\quad}$

$A = \underline{\quad}$

> **Connect to Vocabulary**
>
> You can also write the formula for the area (A) of a rectangle as $A = b \times h$. Think of the **base** (b) of a rectangle as the measure of any side. The **height** (h) of the rectangle is the measure of a side perpendicular to the base.

G. The rectangle has an area of _____ square units.

Step It Out

5 meters

HAWKS

7 meters

#1!

2 The Hawks' fans are making a giant banner for a competition. The banner has the dimensions shown. What is the area of the banner?

A. Write the formula that you can use to solve the problem.

Formula: _____ = _____ × _____

$A =$ _____ × _____

B. Write the measure of the length, *l*, and the width, *w*, of the banner.

$A =$ _____

C. Find the area of the banner.

D. The area of the banner

is _____ square meters.

The area of a rectangle with length and width measured in meters is given in square meters.
1 meter × 1 meter = 1 square meter

Turn and Talk How would the area of the banner change if the banner was turned so that the width is 7 meters and the length is 5 meters?

Check Understanding Math Board

1 Mr. Nielsen is going to buy sod for a portion of his yard, but first, he must know the area of the surface that he wants to cover. What is the area? 18 feet

25 feet

Mr. Nielsen's yard

_____

Find the area.

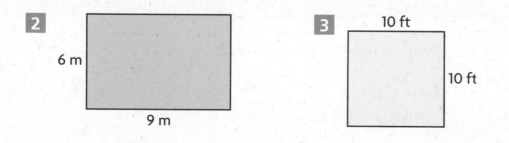

2

6 m

9 m

3 10 ft

10 ft

On Your Own

4 Jason has a sticker on a folder. What is the area of the sticker?

_____

7 cm

BE AWESOME!

3 cm

5 Lisa is setting square tiles on a backsplash. What is the area of each tile?

_____

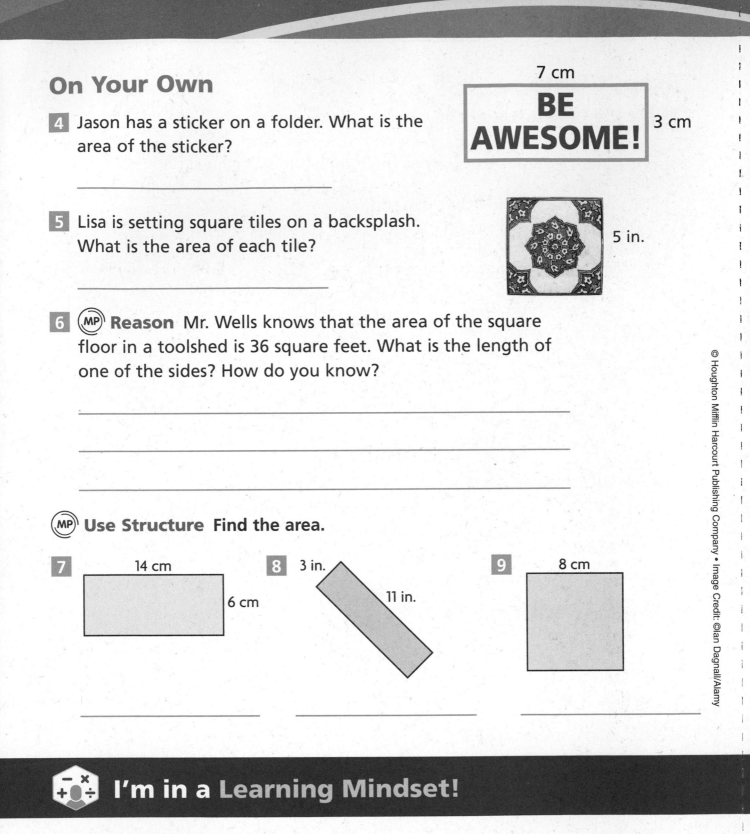

5 in.

6 (MP) **Reason** Mr. Wells knows that the area of the square floor in a toolshed is 36 square feet. What is the length of one of the sides? How do you know?

_____

_____

_____

(MP) **Use Structure** Find the area.

7

14 cm

6 cm

_____

8

3 in.

11 in.

_____

9

8 cm

_____

🔢 I'm in a Learning Mindset!

What parts of solving problems using the area formula am I comfortable with?

_____

_____

Name _____

Find the Area of Combined Rectangles

(I Can) find the area of a figure made of combined rectangles.

Step It Out

1 Brody and his dad are designing a tree house. The diagram shows the shape of the floor. What is the total area of the floor?

You can use addition to find the total area of the combined rectangles.

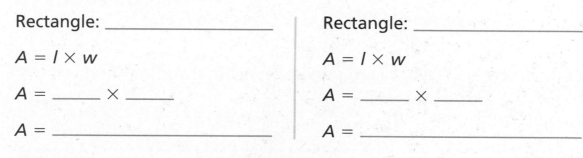

A. Label each rectangle. Use the area formula to find the area of each rectangle.

Rectangle: _____   Rectangle: _____

$A = l \times w$ $A = l \times w$

$A = $ _____ $\times$ _____ $A = $ _____ $\times$ _____

$A = $ _____ $A = $ _____

B. Add the areas to find the total area.

_____ + _____ = _____

C. The total area of the floor of the tree house

in square feet (sq ft) is _____.

Turn and Talk If a line is drawn to separate the figure in a different place, how does the area change?

Step It Out

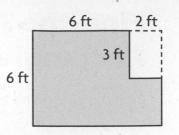

2 Brody cut an opening for a window in the wall of the tree house. What is the area of the wall?

6 ft

You can use subtraction to find the area of the combined rectangles.

A. Use the area formula to find the area of each rectangle.

Area of the whole wall	**Area of the window**
$A = l \times w$	$A = l \times w$
$A = $ _____ $\times$ _____	$A = $ _____ $\times$ _____
$A = $ _____ sq ft	$A = $ _____ sq ft

B. Subtract the areas to find the area of the wall.

_____ $-$ _____ $=$ _____

C. The area of the wall is _____ square feet.

 **Turn and Talk** What is another way that you can find the area of the wall?

Check Understanding Math Board

Find the area of the shaded part of the figure.

1

9 cm

4 cm

4 cm

9 cm

2

10 ft

2 ft

5 ft

9 ft

On Your Own

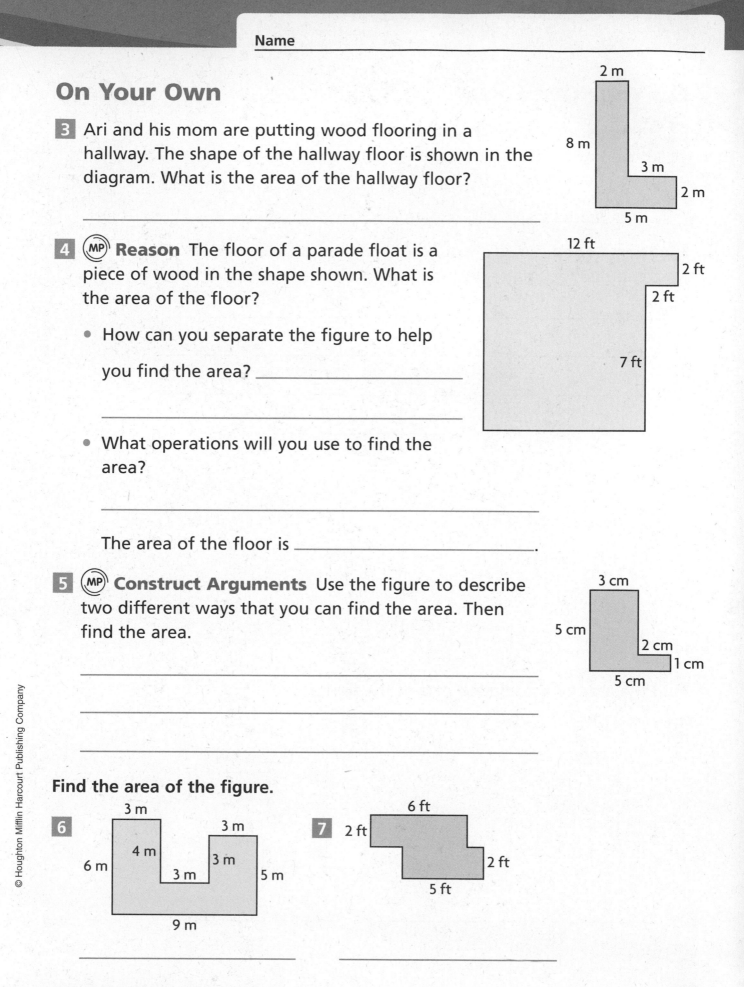

3 Ari and his mom are putting wood flooring in a hallway. The shape of the hallway floor is shown in the diagram. What is the area of the hallway floor?

_____

4 (MP) **Reason** The floor of a parade float is a piece of wood in the shape shown. What is the area of the floor?

- How can you separate the figure to help

  you find the area? _____

  _____

- What operations will you use to find the area?

  _____

  The area of the floor is _____.

5 (MP) **Construct Arguments** Use the figure to describe two different ways that you can find the area. Then find the area.

_____

_____

_____

Find the area of the figure.

6

7

On Your Own

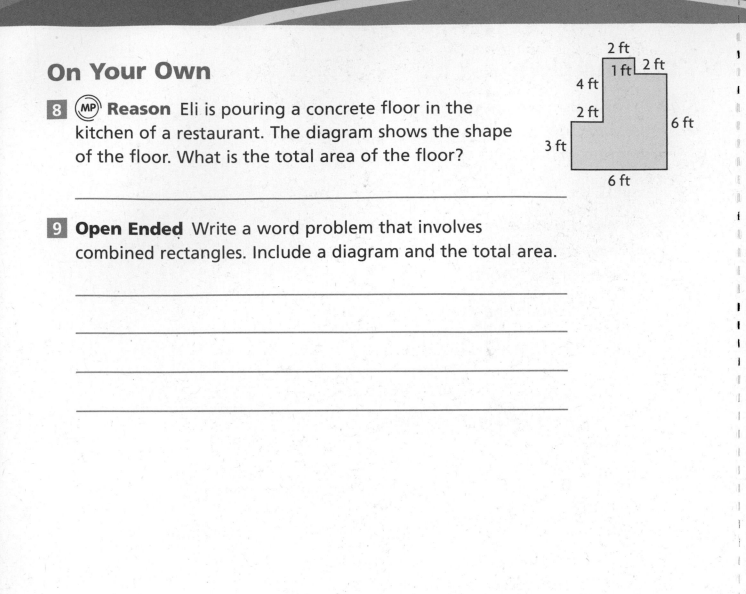

8 (MP) **Reason** Eli is pouring a concrete floor in the kitchen of a restaurant. The diagram shows the shape of the floor. What is the total area of the floor?

_____

9 **Open Ended** Write a word problem that involves combined rectangles. Include a diagram and the total area.

_____

_____

_____

Find the area of the shaded part of the figure.

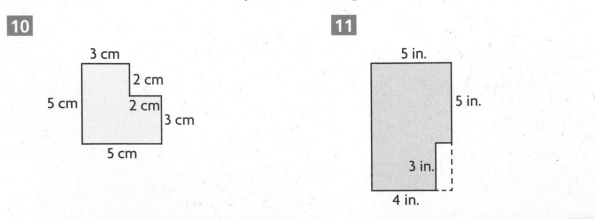

10

3 cm
2 cm
5 cm
2 cm
3 cm
5 cm

_____

11

5 in.
5 in.
3 in.
4 in.

_____

Name _____

Find Unknown Measures

(**I Can**) find the unknown measure of a rectangle given the length of one side and the area or perimeter.

Step It Out

1 ▸ Leisl is decorating the front window of a shop with a string of lights. She uses 50 feet of lights around the window. The window is 10 feet wide. What is the length of the window?

A. What do you want to find out? _____

B. What do you know?

_____

_____

C. Use the perimeter formula to find the unknown. Write *l* for the unknown.

$$P \ = \ 2 \ \times \ l \ + \ 2 \ \times \ w$$

_____ = _____ × _____ + _____ × _____

_____ = _____ × _____ + _____

D. $2 \times l$ is an unknown addend. How can you use the equation to find $2 \times l$? _____

$2 \times l =$ _____

$2 \times$ _____ $= 30$ What number multiplied by 2 is 30?

$l =$ _____

E. The length of the window is _____ feet.

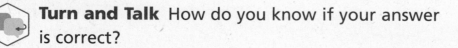 **Turn and Talk** How do you know if your answer is correct?

Step It Out

2 Samuel is decorating a different window in the shop. The window is a rectangle and has an area of 72 square feet. The length of the window is 9 feet. What is the width?

A. What do you want to find out?

_____

B. What do you know?

_____

_____

C. Use the area formula to find the unknown. Write *w* for the unknown measure.

$$A = l \times w$$

_____ = _____ × _____   What number multiplied by 9 is 72?

$w =$ _____

D. The width of the window is _____.

 Turn and Talk How can you find the area of a square with a side that measures 5 inches?

Check Understanding [Math Board]

Use the area or perimeter formula to find the unknown measure.

1 Elise is painting a stage set that has an area of 48 square feet. The width of the set is 6 feet. What is the length?

_____

2 Jada has 38 yards of fencing to put around a paddock for some goats. She has the length set as 10 yards. What is the width of the paddock?

_____

On Your Own

3 Cameron is digging up a section of grass to plant a vegetable garden. The garden will be 30 feet long and have a perimeter of 80 feet.

How wide will the garden be? _____

4 Jackie is marking off a section of a yard to practice field hockey. The area of the section is 56 square meters. The length is 8 meters. What is the width of the section?

_____

5 (MP) **Reason** The square-shaped plaza at the center of a small village has an area of 100 square meters. How can you find the length of one side of the plaza?

_____

_____

_____

(MP) **Use Structure** Use the area or perimeter formula to find the unknown measure.

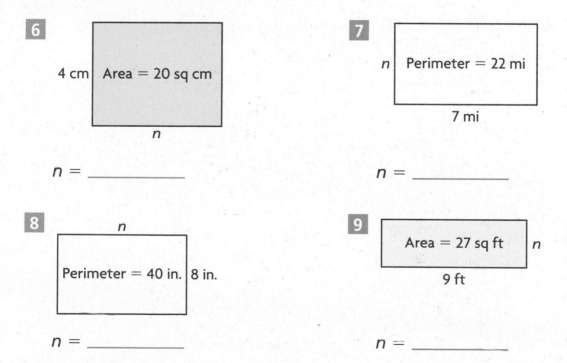

6

4 cm | Area = 20 sq cm

n

n = _____

7

n | Perimeter = 22 mi

7 mi

n = _____

8

n

Perimeter = 40 in. | 8 in.

n = _____

9

Area = 27 sq ft | *n*

9 ft

n = _____

On Your Own

10 **History** Checkers is one of the oldest board games still played today. The oldest known checkerboard is over 5,000 years old. A standard checkerboard is square and has an area of 64 square inches. What is the length of one side

of the board? _____

11 **Open Ended** Write a word problem that involves finding an unknown measure of a rectangle given an area or a perimeter and one length. Include a diagram and the answer.

_____

_____

_____

12 (MP) **Use Structure** A square has a perimeter of 24 inches. How can you find the length of a side?

_____

_____

(MP) **Use Structure** Use the area or perimeter formula to find the unknown measure.

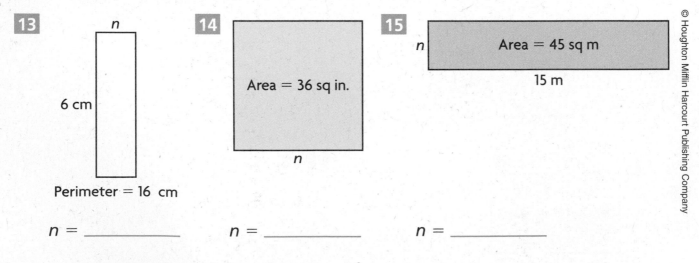

13

n

6 cm

Perimeter = 16 cm

$n =$ _____

14

Area = 36 sq in.

n

$n =$ _____

15

n Area = 45 sq m

15 m

$n =$ _____

Name _____

Solve Area Problems

(**I Can**) find the area of a rectangular region that is formed by taking away rectangular pieces from its interior.

Step It Out

1 Josh runs a glass-bottom boat touring business. He wants to install a non-slip surface on the walkway of the deck. What is the area of the walkway that needs the non-slip surface?

Glass-Bottom Boat Diagram

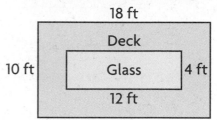

A. What do you know?

_____

_____

B. How can you solve the problem?

_____

_____

Glass	**Deck**
$A = l \times w$	$A = l \times w$
$A = $ _____ $\times$ _____	$A = $ _____ $\times$ _____
$A = $ _____	$A = $ _____

C. Subtract the area of the glass from the area of the deck.

D. The area of the walkway that needs

the non-slip surface is _____.

 Turn and Talk What did you do to help make sense of the problem?

Step It Out

Glass-Bottom Boat Diagram

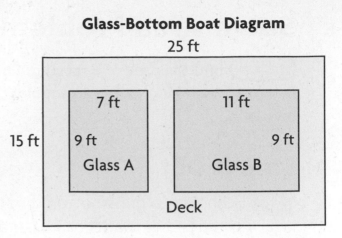

2 Josh has a second glass-bottom boat with two viewing areas. He wants to install a non-slip surface on the walkway of the deck. What is the area of the walkway that needs the non-slip surface?

A. What do you know?

_____

_____

B. How can you solve the problem?

_____

_____

Glass A	Glass B	Deck
$A = l \times w$	$A = l \times w$	$A = l \times w$
$A = $ _____ $\times$ _____	$A = $ _____ $\times$ _____	$A = $ _____ $\times$ _____
$A = $ _____	$A = $ _____	$A = $ _____

C. Add the areas of the glass, then subtract the sum from the area of the deck.

D. The area of the walkway that needs

the non-slip surface is _____.

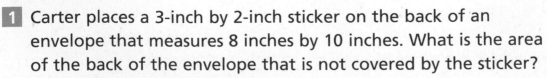

Check Understanding 　Math Board

1 Carter places a 3-inch by 2-inch sticker on the back of an envelope that measures 8 inches by 10 inches. What is the area of the back of the envelope that is not covered by the sticker?

_____

On Your Own

2 Chloe is building a wooden bench around a tree. The space for the tree is a square with a side length of 4 feet. The bench will be a rectangle that measures 12 feet by 14 feet.

What is the area of the bench? _____

(MP) Use Structure Find the area of the shaded part of the rectangle.

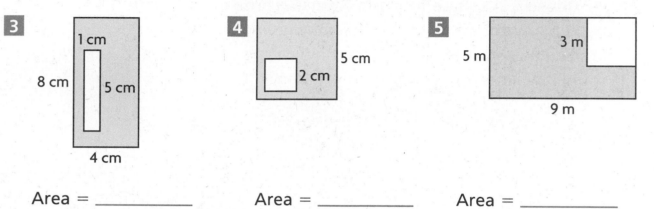

3
1 cm
8 cm
5 cm
4 cm

4
5 cm
2 cm

5
3 m
5 m
9 m

Area = _____   Area = _____   Area = _____

6 The central chamber of the Lincoln Memorial is 74 feet long and 60 feet wide. Lincoln's statue sits on a pedestal that is 17 feet long and 16 feet wide. What is the area of the central chamber that surrounds the pedestal?

_____

7 **STEM** An electrician is installing a wall plate for a double light switch like the one shown. The wall plate is 12 centimeters by 13 centimeters. Each hole for the light toggle measures 1 centimeters by 2 centimeters. What is the area of the wall plate, not including

the holes? _____

8 Brett wants to hang wallpaper on a rectangular wall that measures 8 feet by 14 feet. The wall has a window with an area of 4 square feet. What is the area of the wall that Brett wants to wallpaper?

_____

On Your Own

9 Owen is painting a wall. The wall has a window and a door, as shown in the diagram. What is the area of the wall not including the window and the door? _____

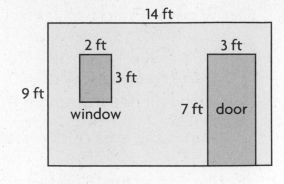

10 (MP) **Reason** A square fountain covers an area of 25 square meters. A plaza surrounds it. The total area of the plaza is 4 times the area of the fountain. How can you find the area of the plaza not covered by the fountain?

_____

_____

_____

11 Laura is designing a square flower garden. The outer edge will have blue flowers, then there will be purple flowers, and the middle will have yellow flowers. How can you find the area that will only have yellow and blue flowers?

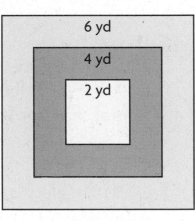

_____

_____

_____

(MP) **Use Structure** Find the area of the shaded part of the rectangle.

12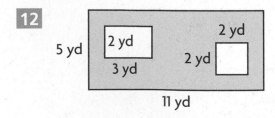

Area = _____

13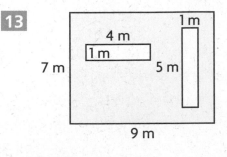

Area = _____

Vocabulary

1 Draw and label a rectangle using the terms in the vocabulary box.

Vocabulary

base
height

Concepts and Skills

2 (MP) **Use Tools** Max is marking off a rectangular section of the gym floor to practice bowling. The section has an area of 48 square meters and a length of 8 meters.

What is the width? Tell what strategy or tool you will use to answer the question, explain your choice, and then find the width.

_____

_____

3 Which is the area of the shaded part of the rectangle?

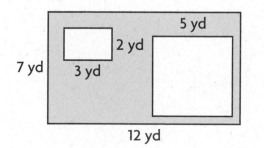

5 yd

2 yd

7 yd   3 yd

12 yd

(A) 31 sq yd   (C) 59 sq yd

(B) 53 sq yd   (D) 109 sq yd

4 Shana is building a deck around a tree. She will cut a square space for the tree that has a side length of 3 feet. The deck will be a rectangle that measures 10 feet by 12 feet. What is the area of the deck?

_____

Find the area of the shaded part of the figure.

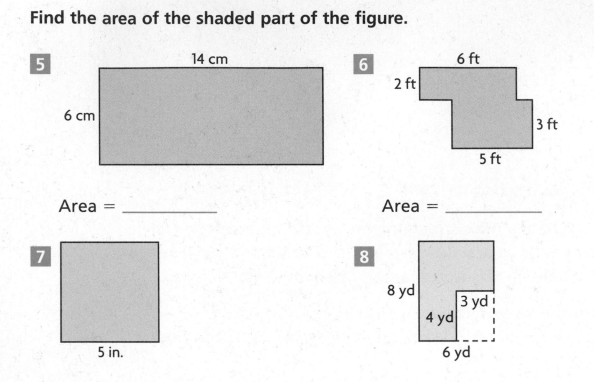

5
14 cm
6 cm

Area = _____

6
6 ft
2 ft
3 ft
5 ft

Area = _____

7
5 in.

Area = _____

8
8 yd
4 yd
3 yd
6 yd

Area = _____

9 Use the perimeter formula, $P = 2 \times l + 2 \times w$, to find the unknown measure.

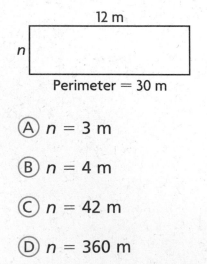

12 m
n
Perimeter = 30 m

Ⓐ $n = 3$ m

Ⓑ $n = 4$ m

Ⓒ $n = 42$ m

Ⓓ $n = 360$ m

Index

Index

N

O

Index

operations *(continued)*
  regroup for, 117–120, 121–124, 203–206
  represent, 101–104
  subtraction
    of angles, 349–352, 353–356
    division as repeated subtraction,
      149–152
    estimate differences, 35–38
    of fractions, 375–378, 379–382,
      391–394, 413–416
    of mixed numbers, 391–394, 399–404,
      405–408, 413–416
    of whole numbers, 35–38, 39–42

order
  data, on line plots, 507–510
  fractions, 291–294
  by place value, 19–22
  property of. *See* Commutative Property
    of Addition; Commutative Property of
    Multiplication

order of operations, 127

ounces (oz), 491–492, 499–502

P

parallel lines, 445–448, 457–460

parallelogram, 457–460

partial products, 109–112, 113–116,
  195–198, 199–202, 207–210

partial quotients, 153–156

patterns
  defined, 259
  number, 259–262
  of products, 77–80
  of quotients, 81–84
  shape, 479–482

perimeter of rectangle, 43–46

period, in a multi-digit number, 7

perpendicular lines, 445–448, 457–460

pints (pt), 490, 503–506

place value
  compare and order by, 19–22
  of decimals, 299–302, 303–306, 311–314
  defined, 5–7

to divide, 165–170, 171–174
to multiply, 117–120, 121–124, 211–214
product patterns and, 77–80
quotient patterns and, 81–84
regroup by, 15–18. *See also* regroup
relationships, 5–10, 11–14
rounding and, 23–26. *See also* rounding

points, 327–330

polygon, 449–452, 457–460, 473–478

pounds (lb), 491–492, 499–502

prerequisite skills. *See also* Are You Ready?
  for addition, 30
  for angles, 326
  for area, 218
  for decimals, 298
  for division, 132, 160
  for estimation, 76
  for fractions, 266, 298, 362, 390, 420
  for lines of symmetry, 468
  for measurement, 488, 514
  for multiplication, 100, 184
  for number theory, 240
  for patterns, 468
  for place value, 4
  for problem situations, 52
  for subtraction, 30
  for time, 534
  for two-dimensional figures, 444

prime numbers, 255–258

problem solving
  comparison problems. *See* comparison
    problems
  multistep problems. *See* multistep
    problems

products. *See also* multiplication
  estimate, 85–88, 189–194, 207–210
  partial, 109–112, 113–116, 195–198,
    199–202, 207–210

properties of operations
  Associative Property of Addition,
    409–412
  Associative Property of Multiplication,
    94, 187
  Commutative Property of Addition,
    409–412

Commutative Property of Multiplication, 93

Distributive Property, 105–108, 110–111, 145–148, 197

Q

quadrilateral, 457–460

quarts (qt), 490, 503–506

quotients. *See also* division
check, 171–174
defined, 247
estimate, 89–92
partial, 153–156
place value in, 165–170

R

rays, 327–330

reasonableness of answers
of differences, 35–38
of multistep problems, 128, 176, 211–214
of products, 85–88, 114, 115, 118, 120, 203–205, 207, 208
of quotients, 89–92, 172
of sums, 31–34

rectangle
area of, 219–222, 223–226, 227–230, 231–234
attributes of, 457–460
perimeter formula for, 43–46, 227–230

reflex angles, 341

regroup
defined, 16
to divide, 161–164, 166–167
to multiply, 117–120, 121–124, 203–206
to rename numbers, 15–18
to subtract, 35–38

regular octagon, 473–478

regular polygon, 474–476, 482

remainders, 137–140, 141–144, 172, 176

rename
fractions, 308–310, 315, 383–386, 395–398

mixed numbers, 402, 405–408, 436
whole numbers, 15–18, 83, 186–187

repeated subtraction, 149–152

represent
addition, 31–32
angles, 327–330, 335–336, 339, 345–346, 348
area, 219
comparison problems, 39–40, 53–56, 57–60, 61–64, 65–68
composite numbers, 255
customary measurement units, 490–491, 493–494, 496–497, 499–500, 502, 503–504
division
Distributive Property and, 145–148
with equal groups, 133–136
partial quotients, 153–154
patterns, 81–82
place value and, 165–167
regrouping, 161–164
remainders, 137–140, 141–142
as repeated subtraction, 149
equivalent fractions as decimals, 307–308
estimations, 85–87, 89, 189
factors, 241–244, 245–246, 249
fractions
add, 367–370, 371–374
compare, 267–270, 271–274, 288, 290, 293
decompose, 363–366
equivalent, 275–278, 281–282
multiply, 422–424, 425–428, 429–431
subtract, 375–378, 379–381
hundredths, 303–306
lines, 329–330, 445, 447–448
lines of symmetry, 469–472, 473–478
metric measurement units, 515–517, 519–520, 523–524
mixed number addition and subtraction, 391–392, 399–404, 405–406
money, 315–318, 319
multiplication
Distributive Property and, 105–108
with equal groups, 101–104

© Houghton Mifflin Harcourt Publishing Company

Index

represent (continued)
    expanded form for, 109–110
    by multiples of ten, 185–186
    with partial products, 113–114,
      195–198, 199
    patterns, 77–78
    by place value, 117–119, 121–122
    prime numbers, 255
    renaming, 395–396, 398, 405–406
    shape patterns, 479–480
    subtraction, 35–36
    tenths, 299–302
    time, 535, 539–542
    whole numbers, 5–7, 11–12, 15–17, 19,
      21, 23–24

rhombus, 457–460

right angles, 341, 344, 353, 356,
    446–447, 449–450, 457–460, 464

right triangle, 449–452

rounding
    to add, 32–34
    defined, 24
    to divide, 89–92
    to multiply, 85–88, 126, 190–194
    place value and, 23–26
    to subtract, 36–38

S

scalene triangle, 453–456

seconds, 535–538, 539–542, 543–546

shape patterns, 479–482

square, 222, 229–230, 233–234, 457–460,
    474, 477

square unit, 219–222

standard form, 11–14

STEM Task, 1, 14, 38, 49, 72, 96, 174, 181,
    188, 233, 237, 261, 278, 302, 348, 359,
    386, 416, 441, 448, 459, 476, 485, 498,
    526, 530

straight angles, 341

subtraction
    of angles, 350–352, 353–356
    division as repeated subtraction, 149–152

estimate differences, 36–38
    of fractions, 375–378, 379–382, 391–394,
      413–416
    of mixed numbers, 391–394, 401–404,
      405–408, 414–416
    of whole numbers, 35–38, 39–42

sums, 31–34. *See also* addition

symmetry, lines of, 469–472, 473–478, 479

T

Table of Measures. *See More Practice
and Homework Journal*

tally table, 507, 509–510

technology and digital resources.
See Ed: Your Friend in Learning for
    interactive instruction, interactive
    practice, and videos.

tens patterns, 77–80, 81–84

tenths, 299–303

term, of patterns, 259–262

thousands patterns, 77–80

time
    compare units of, 535–538, 547, 549–550
    elapsed, 534, 539–542, 543–547, 550
    end, 543–547
    start, 543–547

tons (T), 491–492, 499, 501–502

trapezoid, 457–460, 473–478

triangle, 449–452, 453–456, 461, 464,
    473–474, 476, 479–482

two-dimensional figures
    angles of, 449–452, 457–460,
      461–464
    area
      of combined shapes, 223–226,
        231–234
      defined, 220
      formula, 219–222
      problem solving with, 231–234
      of rectangle, 219–222, 223–226,
        227–230, 231–234
      unknown measures and, 227–230
    lines of symmetry for, 473–478